2020 Makeover

Your Astrology for a New Beginning

by Guru Rattana, Ph.D.

Published by Yoga Technology, LLC

www.yogatech.com

websales@yogatech.com

PO Box 443, Sunbury, PA 17801

Phone: (570) 988 4680, Fax: (570) 988-4640

Front cover artwork by Chris Stell
The cover picture is a seasonal astronomical depiction of
the movement of the constellations around the zodiac.

Back cover photo by Yulia Sokirko
Editing and page layout by Chris Zook

First Edition
ISBN: 978-1-888029-25-3

Copyright © 2019 Guru Rattana, Ph.D.

All rights reserved. No part of this publication may be reproduced, stored in a retrieval system, or transmitted in any form or by any means, electronic, mechanical, photocopying, recording, or otherwise, without the prior written permission of the publisher.

Table of Contents

INTRODUCTION 3
    Organization and How to Use This Book 4
    My Mother Ruth — Saturn, Pluto, and Sun Conjunct 6
    Many Stories, Many Stages 7

CHAPTER 1: THE LANGUAGE OF ASTROLOGY 8
    Symbols and Archetypes 8
    The 10 Universal Energies 9
    Energetic Anatomy of Zodiac Archetypes... 11
    The Five Basics of Astrology 12
    Transits Are Moving Parts 14

CHAPTER 2: WHAT IS HAPPENING IN 2020? 16
    Summary of the Three New Cycles 18

CHAPTER 3: THREE CONJUNCTIONS AND NEW CYCLES 22
    The Saturn and Pluto Conjunction: January 12, 2020 22
    Previous Saturn-Pluto Conjunctions 25
    Saturn-Pluto in Capricorn: 1518 and 2020 26
    The 2020 Jupiter-Pluto Cycle: Spring 2020 29
    The Aquarius Jupiter-Saturn Cycle: Dec. 21, 2020 30
    Jupiter-Saturn Cycles Shift from the Earth to Air Signs.. 32

CHAPTER 4: A DEEPER LOOK AT THE 2020 ALIGNMENTS 34
    Signs of the Breakdown of Collective Institutions 36
    Challenges and Opportunities 38

CHAPTER 5: WHERE ARE THE OTHER PLANETS IN 2020? 41
    Neptune in Pisces 41
    Uranus in Taurus 42
    North Node in Cancer and South Node in Capricorn... 43
    Chiron in Aries 45
    Mars in Aries for Six Months 47

CHAPTER 6: YOUR SOUL PATH ASTROLOGY FOR 2020 AND BEYOND 48
    Personal — How Will All This Play Out? 48
    Optimizing Jupiter ♃ 49
    Optimizing Saturn ♄ 51
    Optimizing Pluto ♇ 53
    Embracing Your Personal Journey 54

CHAPTER 7: NEW BEGINNINGS FOR THE 12 SIGNS 57

CHAPTER 8: THE ACTIVATING ANGLES IN YOUR HOROSCOPE 59

CHAPTER 9: HOW TO READ YOUR BIRTH CHART AND TRANSITS 63
    How to Read Your Chart and Transits... 63
    Who Is Impacted When? 65

ANNOUNCING YOUR NEW BEGINNING 65
1 DEGREE AQUARIUS 68

CHAPTER 10: LIVING AND AWAKENING WITH SATURN AND PLUTO 69

SATURN AND PLUTO 70
A REALISTIC APPROACH TO LIFE 71
OUR PERSONAL LIFE JOURNEY 71
SATURN TRANSITS: REALISTIC MANAGEMENT OF OUR LIFE 73
PLUTO TRANSITS 76

CHAPTER 11: SATURN AND PLUTO THROUGH THE HOUSES AND SIGNS 77

FIRST HOUSE/ARIES: IDENTITY AND PERSONAL EXISTENCE 80
SECOND HOUSE/TAURUS: SELF-VALUE AND TAKING CARE OF OURSELVES 82
THIRD HOUSE/GEMINI: INFORMATION AND ACTIVITIES 84
FOURTH HOUSE/CANCER: EMOTIONAL BEING, INNER FOUNDATION 87
FIFTH HOUSE/LEO: MINING AND ENJOYING OUR GIFTS 90
SIXTH HOUSE/VIRGO: CONSOLIDATE AN INDEPENDENT SELF 93
SEVENTH HOUSE/LIBRA: PERSONAL RELATIONSHIPS 95
EIGHTH HOUSE/SCORPIO: CYCLES, DEATH, AND REBIRTH 100
NINTH HOUSE/SAGITTARIUS: HIGHER DETACHED PERSPECTIVE 103
TENTH HOUSE/CAPRICORN: WE ARE TESTED IN THE WORLD 105
ELEVENTH HOUSE/AQUARIUS: HOW WE CREATE TOGETHER 108
TWELFTH HOUSE/PISCES: CONNECTION TO A HIGHER POWER 111

CHAPTER 12: 2020 IS A NEW BEGINNING 115

APPENDIX 1: UNDERSTANDING YOUR BIRTH CHART 120

OUR SUN AND MOON 123
THE PERSONAL INNER PLANETS 124
TRANSITIONAL PLANETS, CHIRON, AND THE NODES 124
IMPERSONAL OUTER PLANETS 125
ASCENDANT AND ANGLES 126

APPENDIX 2: DECODE YOUR ENERGETIC BLUEPRINT 128

ENERGETIC ANATOMY OF ZODIAC ARCHETYPES 129

ABOUT GURU RATTANA, PH.D. 131

BOOKS BY GURU RATTANA, PH.D. 132

Introduction

Welcome to an adventure of a lifetime — 2020 and the decade of the 2020s on planet Earth!

Your Life in the 2020 Decade

It seems hard to believe but the third decade of the 21st century is now! The year 2020 is an extraordinary year when the choices we make will determine our fate, destiny, and life path.

We live in an era of extreme polarization, which is driven in part by dogmatic adherence to our own views and harsh judgment of others who don't agree with us. Beyond the conflict of duality lies the gift of being given a choice. As we move into the next decade, the most important choice we can make relates to how we wish to orient ourselves and our life journey. The pivotal questions we can ask ourselves are

- ♥ How do I want to live my life in the next 10 years and beyond?
- ♥ What attitude is going to benefit me, my family and friends, and the world?
- ♥ Where do I want to be at (insert your age) in 2030?

A 10-Year Plan/Attitude

Setting realistic and heartfelt goals is important. Although we can't know what exactly will happen, or control specific outcomes, whatever we wish to accomplish will be influenced by our attitude and our consciousness. We can certainly choose our attitude and work toward a more awakened heart-centered consciousness.

- ♥ We can make kindness our baseline instead of criticism and judgment.
- ♥ We can orient ourselves with our heart and choose compassion over conflict.
- ♥ We can make choices that optimize our physical, mental, and emotional health.
- ♥ We can choose gratitude for what we have and who we are.
- ♥ We can serve love and offer our gifts to those who can benefit.
- ♥ We can leverage what we have and be authentic and honest with ourselves.
- ♥ We can have fun exploring our creativity and embracing our unique life.

Rare Planetary Alignments

We don't need astrology to know that something very big is happening. However, we can use astrology to confirm our feelings and to probe deeper into the dynamics of the current events in both our personal and collective lives.

When rare planetary lineups happen, we can look to the past to see if significant changes coincided with them in a previous era. Did you know that 502 years ago on October 31, 1517, Martin Luther posted his 95 Theses on the door of the Catholic church in Germany? This was the event that precipitated the Protestant Reformation and led to profound political, social, and religious shifts and wars that forever changed the power structures in Europe and beyond.

Ferdinand Pauwels, *Luther Hammers His 95 Theses to the Church Door*, oil on canvas, 1872. Collection: Eisenach, Wartburg-Stiftung. Image: Wikimedia Commons.

Luther's audacious act, which would transform the world, took place in the two-month run up to a Pluto-Saturn conjunction in Capricorn in January 1518.

Guess what? On January 12, 2020, Pluto and Saturn meet again in Capricorn! (Discussed in detail in chapter 3.)

This time, we won't be writing out our "theses" by hand and posting them on a church door. Not just one single individual will be offering carefully considered thoughts about how powerful institutions administer their affairs. Now millions of people want to be heard and are posting their views (thoughtful and revengeful, caring and crazy, fake and authentic, honest and deceptive, and everything else) daily on the Internet.

Watch your screens instead of church doors for instantaneous updates on what could be the biggest mass movement the world has ever seen. Some say the world will never be the same. We are both witnesses and participants.

Organization and How to Use This Book

Because this book contains many details and in-depth investigations about major astrological events occurring over the next year, I suggest a slow careful read, especially for those less proficient in astrology. Focus on what is most relevant to you and helps you better understand and deal with your life. This book is designed to guide you through 2020 and the 2020 decade, so keep it handy and let it enrich your life journey.

Chapter 1 — The Language of Astrology
Offers a primer (or refresher) for novices and those new to astrology on the basic components of astrology, its symbology, and astrological archetypes, necessary for understanding the rest of the book.

Additional information about the properties of the planets and zodiac signs are found in **Appendix 1 — Understand Your Birth Chart. Appendix 2 — Decode Your Energetic Blueprint** outlines how to identify your personal formula of the basic universal energies as set out in your birth chart.

Chapter 2 — Brief Summary of 2020 Planetary Alignments
The overview in this chapter can be used as a point of reference for the important 2020 astrological events, including the *what* and the *when*.

Chapter 3 — Three Conjunctions and New Cycles
Explains in more detail the planetary (Pluto, Saturn, Jupiter) and zodiac (Capricorn) components of the three new cycles initiated in the 2020 alignments and gives historical examples of similar alignments in the past.

Chapter 4 — A Deeper Look at the 2020 Alignments
Examines the possible impacts and implications that can help us understand the significance of the 2020 alignments and how we will be affected personally and collectively.

Chapter 5 — Where Are the Other Planets in 2020?
Explains how Neptune, Uranus, Chiron, the North and South Nodes, and Mars are contributing to the overall picture.

Chapter 6 — Your Soul Path Astrology for 2020 and Beyond
Takes things to a more personal level and explores how to appreciate and optimize your life challenges related to Jupiter, Saturn, and Pluto.

Chapter 7 — New Beginnings for the 12 Signs
Offers short descriptions of some of the possible new beginnings related to the 12 zodiac signs.

Chapter 8 — The Activating Angles in Your Horoscope
Explains how to identify and understand the importance of four major points on your birth chart.

Chapter 9 — How to Read Your Birth Chart and Transits
Provides specific directions on how to read your horoscope and identify how the transiting planets are impacting you.

Chapter 10 — Living and Awakening with Saturn and Pluto
Features an in-depth analysis of the Saturn and Pluto archetypes and how they play out in our human experience.

Chapter 11 — Saturn and Pluto Through the Houses and Signs
Explores in detail the challenges and gifts of learning with Saturn and Pluto in the 12 houses and 12 zodiac signs.

Chapter 12 — 2020 Is a New Beginning
Offers reflections on how to approach life during the transition era in which we are currently living.

My Mother Ruth — Saturn, Pluto, and Sun Conjunct

There are many ways that the energies of the zodiac signs and planets play out in both our birth chart and when their moving positions interact with our birth chart.

Saturn and Pluto are major players in the 2020 planetary alignments. Their energies challenge us to mature, become more conscious, and be more authentically ourselves. Those with Saturn and Pluto conjunct when they were born can develop a high level of determination and perseverance. I share the following story about my mother as an example of someone with this configuration who admirably took advantage of challenging situations her whole life.

My mother was born with Saturn and Pluto both conjunct her Sun in Cancer (in the tenth house of Capricorn). She grew up in northern Wisconsin in a poor family. To send her to college during the Great Depression in the 1930s, her aunt had to borrow $50. She majored in mathematics but turned to social work as a career. She was a pioneer in the civil rights movement and always treated everyone with respect.

In her 50s, she developed the same health problems that had led to an early death for both her mother and sister — cancer. She looked for alternatives and discovered yoga. I remember the day I came home for Christmas in 1968 when she asked me, "Guess what I discovered? Yoga!" My response was, "What's yoga?" She became my first yoga teacher. I have practiced every day since. I love feeling good!

My mother Ruth opened the first yoga center in the Midwest (Indiana) and introduced yoga, meditation, Reiki, rebirthing, and much more to a Bible Belt community. She was definitely audacious. She was a warrior woman who dedicated her life to helping others and working for justice and truth.

It was sometime in the 1960s before computers (when birth charts were calculated manually) that an astrologer friend gave her a reading. She told her that on a certain future date things looked really bad and advised her to stay in bed and not leave the house. I assume there were some planetary interactions with Pluto, Saturn, and Mars.

Undaunted by this warning, my mother decided that this would be a very special day in her life. She planned fun and interesting activities and got up early to enjoy a full day. She reported later that she had a very delightful day and went to bed happy and content.

The moral of the story is that we can choose our own attitude and decide how we want to use cosmic energies. In her later years (she lived to 92), people would tell her she was so lucky to be healthy and vital. Her answer was, "It's not luck — it's hard work!"

If my mother were alive today, I am sure she would already be taking advantage of the near Saturn-Pluto conjunctions in 2019 and be planning inspiring and brave innovative projects for 2020.

Many Stories, Many Stages

We each have our own story. I invite you to take your personal story into what you read in this book. Focus on what speaks to you. One nugget that talks to your heart and soul is a great gift. Savor it and be grateful for the increased understanding and wisdom gained about yourself and your life.

Life offers us so many gifts, but which ones do we open, accept, and savor? Open the ones that resonate with the core of your being.

What is relevant when you are in your late 20s is going to be different from when you are in your late 50s and beyond. But at each stage, you can identify life themes and penetrate deeper into how you deal with your life challenges. Enjoy your journey and your unique life!

The pivotal questions for each of us at this time are

- ♦ How do I want to live the next decade of my life (and beyond)?
- ♦ How can I take advantage of the openings in 2020 to release fear-based programming and direct my life from my heart?

Chapter 1: The Language of Astrology

Symbols and Archetypes

Astrology invites us to open our mind to another type of knowing that doesn't operate through logical thinking and analysis. Beyond proven or disproven facts lies a realm of understanding that operates through — and increases — intuition, awareness, and awakening of consciousness.

Astrology is a gift granted by the Universe and developed by humans to understand themselves and their journey on planet Earth. The goal of astrology is not fortune telling or foreseeing a prescribed future, but to understand how to more effectively navigate our life by taking advantage of and living in harmony with ever-changing universal energies.

When we observe our life from the perspective of soul awakening, we can use astrology to tune in to the deep pulses of our life and access the deeper meaning and gifts in our life experiences.

Personified Planets and Signs

Astrology speaks to us via symbols and archetypes. Each planet represents a unique configuration of aspects of the human psyche. Each zodiac sign represents ways that we express, understand, and use universal energies.

It can sound a bit strange to personify the planets and to say, for example, "Pluto teaches us...." How can it be that a planet we can't even see teaches us something? Throughout this book, the names of the planets and zodiac signs are simply used as shorthand designations for a host of energies, qualities, and experiences that lead us to investigate our human condition, makeup, and journey. For instance, we say "Pluto" to represent the aspect of our psyche that simultaneously deals with our unconscious, subconscious, conditioning, and soul trying to show us our hidden agendas so that we can release fear and wake up to love.

As you will see, the definition of each of the planets and zodiac signs and how these archetypes work through and for us are endless. We are not looking for definitive answers. We are engaging in an exploration of our being, life, and how we interact with cosmic forces.

Archetypal Principles

In astrology, each planet and its associated zodiac sign represent a fundamental, or archetypal, principle and power. The designation "archetypal" means that these forces are universal and manifest throughout the cosmos and within the human psyche. They define and impel evolutionary change at the personal, global, and cosmic levels. They express at all levels of consciousness and in all manifested forms.[1] The human mind and being operate in the context of these archetypal themes, which underlie and determine the many aspects of our complex mode of operation, including the nature of our personal urges, desires, and perception of reality.

Study of the planets and zodiac signs gives us a structure to investigate our unique individual development, experience, perceptions, and orientation in life within the context of a "shared framework of archetypal-cosmological principles," which define the nature of reality and influence how we participate in the cosmic whole.[2]

Understanding the nature of archetypal energies is pivotal in identifying "the way we are." These energies create certain types of experiences and provoke predictable challenges and lessons that we are given an opportunity to learn this lifetime. In our unconscious state, our subconscious drives us to repeatedly engage in specific patterns of compulsive behavior, luring us into traps that oblige us to transform and evolve. The archetypal powers actually direct us to become more conscious and to upgrade our expression of their energies.[3]

The 10 Universal Energies

There are 10 universal archetypical energies that create life. They are the forces out of which all life is composed. Inherent in the structure of reality, they shape both the human psyche and the cosmos. (The 10 energies are discussed in detail in my recent book *The Inner Art of Kundalini Yoga.*)

The 10 energies are organized into three different categories:

- **2 polarities** (stable/still and moving/flowing)
- **3 phases, or modalities, of creation:** G-O-D (Generating, Organizing, and Deliver/Destroy)
- **5 elements** (earth, water, fire, air, and ether)

Each sign of the zodiac embodies its own combination of energies. For example, Capricorn expresses the moving polarity, the generating phase of creation, and the earth element.

In astrology, we compute only four elements (earth, water, fire, and air), all of which are manifested in physical reality from the universal, nonphysical ether element. Ether is the unifying force that makes it possible for us to experience oneness with everything — when we are balanced and aligned with our soul.

The 10 principal energies offer us an inclusive system for understanding what we are dealing

---

[1] Keiron Le Grice, *The Archetypal Cosmos* (Floris Books, 2010), 280.
[2] Ibid., 285.
[3] Ibid., 250.

with in our life experiences and give us a way to awaken to universal oneness — for we are each a unique manifestation of the same reality from which both the human psyche and the Universe are created. The energies help us identify the formative patterns of the many factors that (1) influence our human experience, (2) shape our personality, and (3) direct, animate, and give meaning to our life challenges.

Each archetypal energy has many facets and ways of manifesting, and each individual has their own personal perspective and expressions. Yet beyond our individual life stories, there are purposeful dynamics that lead us on the evolutionary journey of growth and the awakening to our soul.

Each element, modality, and zodiac sign work with life's challenges in different ways. And, as noted above, each zodiac sign is a unique combination of the two polarities, the three modalities, and the four elements. (See chart below.)

The Zodiac Signs in the Two Polarities

The Universe weaves all creation with *two* basic energies — *one is stable, unchanging and the other is flowing, always moving*. Our soul is made up of the two universal polarities:

(1) The **stable/neutral/mental** polarity expresses through our higher mind, the upper two chakras, and our connection with Spirit. The awakened *stable polarity* allows us to be peaceful, conscious, and intuitive.

(2) The **flowing/evolving/emotional/physical** polarity expresses through our physical body, our emotions, the lower three chakras, and our connection with Mother Earth. The awakened *flowing polarity* allows us to rhythmically flow with the evolutionary cycles of life.

The **air** and **fire** signs are classified as the **stable mental polarity**.
The **earth** and **water** signs are classified as the **flowing feeling polarity**. (See charts below.)

The Zodiac Signs in the Three Modalities

There are four zodiac signs (one from each of the elements) in each of the three modes, or phases, of creation. The astrological designations of G-O-D are G — Cardinal, O — Mutable, D — Fixed.

    G — GENERATING (Cardinal) energies are expressed by
      Aries, Cancer, Libra, and Capricorn

    O — ORGANIZING (Mutable) energies are expressed by
      Gemini, Virgo, Sagittarius, and Pisces

    D — DELIVER (Fixed) energies are expressed by
      Taurus, Leo, Scorpio, and Aquarius

The Zodiac Signs in the Four Elements

Each of the four elements are expressed by three of the zodiac signs (one from each modality).

Earth — Taurus, Virgo, and Capricorn

Water — Cancer, Scorpio, and Pisces

Fire — Aries, Leo, and Sagittarius

Air — Gemini, Libra, and Aquarius

As we learn to tap into the energy and power of each element, we move out of unproductive unconscious expressions into conscious productive expressions of the elements. Below is a brief summary of this process for each element as detailed in *The Inner Art of Kundalini Yoga*.

Earth — from stuck in inertia and depressed to the ability to manifest and deal effectively with worldly concerns

Water — from submerged in emotional drama and immobilized by fear to emotional sensitivity and feeling richness

Fire — from reactive and angry to assertive and courageous with a passion for life

Air — from mental confusion and lost in thoughts to mental clarity and effective communication

Energetic Anatomy of Zodiac Archetypes

Each of the 12 zodiac signs has its own unique combination of the polarities, elements, and modalities.

POLARITIES	STABLE-MENTAL		MOVING-EMOTIONAL/PHYSICAL	
Elements	FIRE	AIR	WATER	EARTH
Modalities				
G—GENERATE	Aries	Libra	Cancer	Capricorn
O—ORGANIZE	Sagittarius	Gemini	Pisces	Virgo
D—DELIVER	Leo	Aquarius	Scorpio	Taurus

The Five Basics of Astrology

Complex and Fascinating

Astrology can seem overwhelming at first because we are confronted with everything at once. Astrology is admittedly complex, but understanding even a few things about the energy dynamics of our soul as set out in our birth chart can be invaluable for deepening our self-understanding. By taking one baby step at a time, we can use this modality as we feel moved to deepen our knowledge of self. There is always more to discover in our journey to explore and love our earthly self and soul. (See Appendix for a discussion of how to decode the basic energies in our birth chart.)

Five Basic Components of Astrology

First, we familiarize ourselves with the basic terms and symbols that represent archetypal energies. Even though these archetypes each have specific definitions, their interpretations are vast and virtually unlimited, making the exploration of our personal journey endless and fascinating!

Though the study of astrology can seem complicated to the beginner, it systematizes and gives us a structure to understand the underlying dynamics of life. There are five basic components of astrology and our birth chart.

1. Zodiac Signs or Archetypes — 12 Energies

Ancient sages, who were acutely attuned to universal energies, divided the sky into 12 areas. They witnessed that the nature of the energies in these different positions in the sky expressed differently in human beings and impacted their behaviors in specific ways. Hence, we have 12 signs or archetypes, each of which embodies its own energy, expresses it in certain ways, and confronts us with unique challenges and gifts (see chart above and summaries below).

2. Planets — Aspects of Our Humanness

In addition to planet Earth, eight major planets revolve around the Sun. Each planet represents an aspect of our humanness and is associated with one of the 12 signs and its archetypal energy.

Each planet also corresponds to one aspect of our human makeup; for example, Mercury represents our mind. (See Appendix for a discussion of each of the planets.)

The planets move through the sky at their own speed, depending on how far away they are from the Sun. As each planet progresses through the sky, it passes through the 12 areas of the zodiac. While the planet is in a particular zodiac arena, it expresses through that energy.

Each sign and planet have their own glyph or symbol. *The key to reading your chart is to first recognize the symbols of the planets and the zodiac signs.*

Asteroids
There are several asteroids, or mini planets, orbiting the Sun that modern astrologers have found useful in furthering our understanding of the dynamics of the human psyche and our life experiences. These include Chiron and Eris, which both add their imprint on the 2020 alignments.

3. Houses — Arenas of Life

The birth chart is divided into 12 houses, which represent the fields or arenas of our life experiences. Each house is associated with one of the 12 zodiac signs.

The birth chart represents the sky and the positions of all the planets in the 12 houses at the moment when we were born. The sign of the zodiac at the horizon at the time of our birth is our rising sign, or ascendant.

The position of each planet in the 12 houses is determined by our ascendant. The placement of the planets in our natal chart indicates the arenas in which this aspect of our being will be challenged and expressed.

4. Aspects — Modes of Interaction

The term *aspects* refers to the energetic relationships between the planets. The primary aspects are *conjunctions* (same sign and degree), *oppositions* (180 degrees apart or opposite each other), *squares* (90 degrees apart), and *trines* (60 degrees apart). The position of the planets in relationship to each other determines how they interact. Their interaction can be harmonious (trines), stimulate action and/or create conflict (squares and oppositions), or stimulate change (all but trines).

5. Transits — Current Planetary Alignments

The term *transits* describes the current, ever-changing planetary positions and how they interact with each other. The energetic effects impact everyone in general and impact us personally according to how these energies interact with the planetary placements in our birth chart.

Planets		Zodiac Signs	
Sun	☉	Aries	♈
Moon	☽	Taurus	♉
Mercury	☿	Gemini	♊
Venus	♀	Cancer	♋
Mars	♂	Leo	♌
Jupiter	♃	Virgo	♍
Saturn	♄	Libra	♎
Uranus	♅	Scorpio	♏
Neptune	♆	Sagittarius	♐
Pluto	♇	Capricorn	♑
Chiron	⚷	Aquarius	♒
North Node	☊	Pisces	♓
South Node	☋		

Axes			
Rising Sign	A^{SC}	Descendent	D^{S}
Midheaven	M^{C}	Nadir (Imum Coeli)	IC

Astrology Chart Guide with Houses, Signs, and Planets

Transits Are Moving Parts

Transits refer to the movements of the planets. For example, if Venus is moving through Taurus, we say Venus is transiting Taurus. It will next transit through Gemini, then Cancer, and make its way through the zodiac.

We look at the zodiac sign, degree, and house placement of the planets in our birth chart and how they match up with the signs and degrees of the transiting planets to identify where and how the transits are impacting our life.

Paying attention to planetary transits helps us understand how our life unfolds. With nudging and support from universal energies, we move through life, take action, and are transformed. Evolution happens.

Monitoring transits and how they impact us helps us use the astrological symbology of cosmic energies to (1) evolve through the stages of life, (2) deepen our sense of self, and (3) awaken to our universal oneness. Becoming more conscious and waking up to universal love are the all-pervasive evolutionary themes.

To investigate how the transiting planets in the 2020 astrological "events" are impacting your life, you will need to have a copy of your birth chart.

See Appendix for tips on how to understand your energy makeup as defined by your birth chart.

Degrees

In addition to the signs of each of the planets, every birth chart also indicates the degree of the sign of each planet. For example, if you were born on the first day that the Sun is in Aries, your Sun would be at 1 degree Aries. If you were born 15 days later, your Sun would be at 15 degrees Aries. If you were born the day before the Sun moved from Aries into Taurus, your Sun would be at 29 degrees Aries. In total, there are 30 degrees for each sign. Thirty degrees becomes the first degree of the following sign.

You need to know the degrees to identify how the moving planets (transits) are interacting with and thus affecting your natal planets.

The first 2020 conjunction happens when Pluto and Saturn are at 23 degrees Capricorn. Thus planets in your birth chart at 23 degrees (or close) will be affected. This is explained in detail in Chapter 9.

Timing of Influence and Orbs

Orbs define the range and intensity of influence of the period that a transit is active or influential in our personal chart. Orbs are measured in degrees.

A planet will begin to influence our natal planets several degrees before it actually aligns with the exact degree. For example, for 23 degrees Capricorn, the orb of influence begins at about 20 degrees. Its influence will diminish or wane as it distances itself. A common orb is 3 to 5 degrees for approaching and up to 3 degrees for separating.

The effects of full Moons can help us understand this concept. The emotional intensity associated with a full Moon often builds several days before the full Moon reaches its peak. The day of the full Moon is the most emotionally intense. There are studies that document how crime rates and crazy happenings increase the day before and on the day of the full Moon. Following the peak (exact time) of the full Moon, we often feel a sense of relief or a letting go, indicating that the orb of influence has passed.

The Moon moves through each sign of the zodiac approximately every two and a half days. Because the Moon moves fast, its orb of influence is very short. The slower the planet, the longer its energy will influence us as it both approaches and passes our natal planets. Its effects will also be longer lasting.

Conjunctions Indicate New Cycles

Conjunction is the name given to the "event" when two or more planets are at the same degree in the same sign. When two or more planets conjunct, they begin a new cycle. As just explained, there is a buildup to the conjunction, which can be felt several degrees before the exact conjunction.

Three conjunctions are the main feature of the 2020 planetary alignments. The most important conjunctions involve at least one outer planet (Uranus, Neptune, and Pluto) and one of the intermediary planets (Saturn and Jupiter). These conjunctions are significant because, as they involve the slower planets, they initiate longer term cycles (at least 20 years) that define trends and themes related to the global collective.

Grand Crosses

Grand crosses are made up of planets positioned with each other at 90 degrees (squares) and 180 degrees (oppositions).

Oppositions can be either conflictual or a source of balance when we call upon the higher expressions of the zodiac pairs (Aries/Libra, Taurus/Scorpio, Gemini/Sagittarius, Cancer/Capricorn, Leo/Aquarius, Virgo/Pisces) to work together.

Squares motivate and prompt us to make choices, take action, and speak our truth. We can't just pretend nothing is happening. Something *is* happening, and we need to deal with whatever it is for us.

Grand crosses happen between zodiac signs in one modality, with one or more planets in each of the four elements.

The planet signs in the Pluto-Saturn grand cross on January 10, 2020, are in cardinal (active) signs (Aries, Cancer, Libra, and Capricorn).

Stellium

Stellium refers to three or more planets in the same sign. The 2020 Pluto-Saturn conjunction January 12, 2020 is made more potent because four planets (a stellium) are conjunct in Capricorn.

Seeing Through the Lens of Astrology

When we study our life through the lens of astrology, we realize that there are many ways that the archetypes can play out, yet life is purposeful, not random. There are many pieces to our own personal puzzle, and they all fit together. There is both order and flexibility. We operate within the boundaries of our own destiny, yet we have free will and choice. There are phases, themes, and progressions that are all circumscribed by divine timing.

Chapter 2:
What Is Happening in 2020?

For years, astrologers have anticipated the year 2020 because it is rare that three new cycles involving the outer planets are initiated in the same year. The last time that Pluto, Saturn, and Jupiter aligned in Capricorn was 502 years ago (October 31, 1517). That date is generally considered the start of the Protestant Reformation, when Martin Luther posted his 95 Theses on the door of the Catholic church in Wittenberg, Germany (see below).

The three 2020 conjunctions indicate that we are entering a new period in history — *the ending of an era and the birth of a new paradigm with respect to both individual and collective power, resources, and consciousness*. Everyone and all levels of society will be affected by the astrological events in 2020.

An overview of the dominant forces can help us understand how we can optimize our use of the powerful cosmic forces unleashed in 2020. Our goal is to take advantage of the openings that are being offered to transform our consciousness and the world.

Astrology Is Not About Forecasting
It is not possible to forecast exactly what is going to happen. However, we can get an idea of how the planetary "events" are influencing our life and present some of the possibilities (both bad and good) of how they may play out. A better understanding can help us be at choice in how to best navigate our personal life.

What Is Going to Happen?

The current state of confusion and chaos in the external world is not going to stop magically overnight. Some things may even get worse. Those who have profited from institutions based on fear, anger, greed, and conflict are going to resist and fight to maintain the status quo, their power, and their privilege.

The good news is that an awakening of our inner world is simultaneously taking place. Millions of people are feeling the heart-centered vibration and tapping into their creativity and desire to share their unique gifts.

What Questions Should We Ask?

In 2018 someone asked me, "When are things going to get better? How about in 2020?" I was honestly taken back by this question. For me, this is the wrong question because it assumes that some planetary events are going to automatically make things change without our participation.

More worthwhile questions include *When are we going to wake up? When are we going to do our part to infuse the planet with love? And what will it take — a catastrophe or a wise, committed choice?*

The Earth is being infused with high-frequency energies that serve as the foundation for the Aquarian Age. The next quantum step in human evolution is our alignment with the vibration of love, which will make it possible to build a heart-centered world. In the vibration of fear, nothing can fundamentally change, only get worse. So if some things look bad, that is because they are.

We can create a new order when enough people value and live from the consciousness of love and peace. Creating a collective consciousness that makes the changes we desire possible requires our active participation in our own awakening and elevating our frequency.

Summary of the Three New Cycles

First, a summary of the significant 2020 astrological "events" that will be discussed in detail throughout the book.

In 2020, three conjunctions involving **Pluto, Saturn,** and **Jupiter** initiate new planetary cycles that will unfold over the next three decades. It is rare that Pluto, Saturn, and Jupiter travel together in the same zone of the zodiac, which is currently Capricorn.

These conjunctions are not merely events to anticipate and live through, and then be grateful that 2020 is over. They will have lasting effects at all levels of our social, political, and economic structures, including global geopolitics and our personal lives. These conjunctions set the tone for an ongoing process that will play out in ways that we cannot know in advance. Much will depend on the level of consciousness of the human players and how we choose to use the energies available to us during this time.

Three New Cycles Begin in 2020

1. **On January 12, 2020, Saturn and Pluto meet in Capricorn (23 degrees) to launch a new 33-year cycle.**
2. **Jupiter and Pluto meet three times in Capricorn (22-24 degrees) in April, June, and November 2020, launching a new 12-year cycle.**
3. **On December 21, 2020, Jupiter and Saturn meet at 1 degree Aquarius, launching a new 20-year cycle.**

The two major zodiac players are **Capricorn** and **Aquarius**. Capricorn represents our collective structures, especially governments and big corporations, and our personal participation in how they are created and sustained. Capricorn is also about our climb up the mountain of life, our soul journey, self-mastery, and our position and contribution in the world.

We get a clearer view of where we are headed in December 2020 when Jupiter and Saturn in

Aquarius begin a new social destiny cycle.

The Major Players and Their Roles

Pluto exposes hidden truths whose concealment causes one to be inauthentic, dishonest, and dysfunctional.

Saturn identifies the practical lessons that we must learn in Earth School and the natural laws that we must obey. Saturn is also about bringing ideas into form.

Jupiter presents us with opportunities and expands our mind so we can see where we are headed and choose our path.

The Players and Their Game

The intensity and impact of the three-planetary rendezvous cannot be underestimated or taken lightly. Next, we look closely at the players and the energies involved.

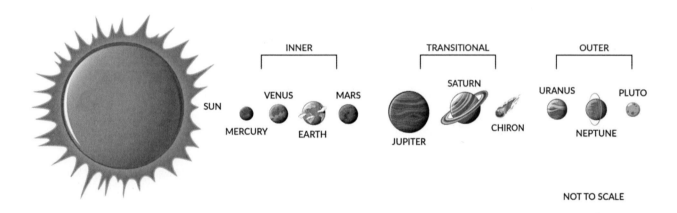

Outer Planet Cycles

The new cycles that begin in 2020 involve **Pluto**, the slowest moving planet, and **Saturn and Jupiter**, the transitional planets, also called the "social structure" or "social destiny" planets that relate to the collective. Saturn and Jupiter orbit between the **slow outer planets (Neptune, Uranus, and Pluto)** and the **faster inner personal planets (Mercury, Venus, and Mars).**

The long-term cycles and interactions of these planets deeply impact our global human experience. Investigation of their archetypal expressions helps us see the bigger picture and gain clarity and understanding of what is transpiring in these chaotic and rapidly changing times.

Pluto Is Deep and Brutally Honest

Pluto, the most distant planet and invisible to the naked eye, exposes the deep hidden complexities in our human psyche that we must face to become emotionally mature adults. Pluto reveals the inner traumas and unconscious conditioning that must be healed if we are to access our inner power.

There is nothing superficial about Pluto. Fantasy and escapism are not tolerated. Pluto requires fundamental change, both personally and collectively. We can be comforted by the fact that Pluto brings to light what must be revealed for us to move forward and to live more conscious, freer, and heart-centered lives.

At the beginning of the Pluto process, we may cling to victimhood or be too naive to know what is going on. At some point, we begin to see and own our dysfunctions and realize that we need to face some uncomfortable feelings and learn some painful lessons. We slowly, and often reluctantly, succumb to the inevitable need to (1) make peace with our past, (2) transform our inner reality, and (3) take responsibility for our own lives.

Our own versions of these lifelong lessons appear in cycles. Each time we confront the "same lessons," we continue our awakening progress. Gradually we gain inner strength, integrity, inner peace, and freedom.

The Pluto process is by its very nature uncomfortable at best, and extremely painful when we resist. Our best strategy is to agree to do what it takes to wake up and face what has been tormenting us for a long time, perhaps our whole life (and past lives). The promise is freedom from inner anxiety and pain. The price is authentic honesty.

Saturn Demands a Serious Reality Check

Saturn is the reality check planet that reminds us that the law of cause and effect directs the show. Saturn is a taskmaster, not a warm fuzzy teddy bear. There is nothing hidden in Saturn's agenda. Everything is on the table — the facts, the resources available — all aspects of physical reality that must be taken into consideration as we deal with the everyday challenges of survival in the physical world.

Jupiter Expands What We Focus On

Jupiter gives us hope that something positive and beneficial can emerge from the arduous process of inner growth and the fundamental changes required by Saturn and Pluto. The Jupiter archetype reminds us that we energize, attract, and expand what we focus on. When Jupiter meets Pluto, it can expand and expose the dark side of what was once hidden. We are well advised to monitor and choose very carefully what we give energy and attention to.

The Jupiter influence can offer openings and opportunities when we maintain a positive attitude and operate from our heart. If we can avoid expanding negativity, scarcity, and fear, Jupiter is available to inspire our future, facilitate our next steps, and help us move on.

Dates and Cycles

Jupiter
Jupiter passes through a zodiac sign every 12–13 months.

Key dates
- **Nov. 8–Dec. 2, 2019**: Jupiter passes through Sagittarius.
- **Dec. 3, 2019–Dec. 20, 2020**: Jupiter transits Capricorn.
- **Dec. 20, 2020–May 13, 2021**: Jupiter enters and remains in Aquarius.

Saturn
Saturn stays in a zodiac sign for two and half to three years and moves through the zodiac in 29 years.

Key dates
- **Dec. 20, 2017–Dec. 16, 2020**: Saturn is in Capricorn.
- **Dec. 17, 2020–Mar. 7, 2023**: Saturn enters Aquarius.

Jupiter + Saturn + Pluto

Key dates
- **Mid-Mar. 2020**: Jupiter approaches Pluto and Saturn.
- **End of Mar. 2020**: Mars joins Saturn and Jupiter in late Capricorn and early Aquarius.
- **Dec. 21, 2020**: Saturn and Jupiter meet at the 1st degree of Aquarius.
    - *The game changes.*

There is nothing superficial about Pluto. Fantasy and escapism are not tolerated. Pluto requires fundamental change, both personally and collectively. We can be comforted by the fact that Pluto brings to light what must be revealed for us to move forward and to live more conscious, freer, and heart-centered lives.

Chapter 3:
Three Conjunctions and New Cycles

In this chapter, we explore in more detail the 2020 conjunctions, drawing on examples in history when the same conjunctions were at play to elucidate potential impacts in the coming years.

The Saturn and Pluto Conjunction: January 12, 2020

The new Saturn-Pluto cycle officially starts at their conjunction on January 12, 2020, at 23 degrees Capricorn. However, we began feeling the powerful disorienting, life-changing effects of the Saturn-Pluto conjunction in 2019.[4]

In 2019, the dynamics of the close interaction between Saturn and Pluto (within 2-3 degrees) were already active and impactful. The intensity increases in December 2019 as the two planets come within 1 degree of each other and then have their exact meeting at 23 degrees on January 12, 2020. The intensity remains very strong at least through January 2020.

Because the Saturn-Pluto conjunction both ends a 38-year cycle and initiates a new 33-year cycle, we may feel like we are in an energetic limbo for several years. (The length of Saturn-Pluto cycles varies because of Pluto's highly elliptical orbit.[5])

In 2020 and for the next few years, we will be experiencing

1. The process of transitioning out of an era
2. The immanence of a new era
3. The recognition of a new period in our life

This new cycle will have a profound global impact, affecting both our personal and collective lives, including political, geopolitical, economic, and environmental impacts.

We will know, or at least deeply sense, a serious shift of direction when both Saturn and Jupiter

---

[4] Information in this section drawn from Jessica Murray, "Seeing the Big Picture: Working with the Transits of 2020," *The Mountain Astrologer*, December 2018–January 2019, 25–32.

[5] Because of its elliptical orbit, Pluto spends a different amount of time in each of the zodiac signs. Pluto spends the longest time in Taurus (32 years). These are the approximate dates of Pluto transits for the past century, which do not indicate when Pluto retrograded back into the previous sign: Pluto in Cancer: 1913–1939 (22 years); Pluto in Leo: 1939–1956 (17 years); Pluto in Virgo: 1956–1972 (16 years); Pluto in Libra: 1972–1984 (12 years); Pluto in Scorpio: 1984–1995 (11 years); Pluto in Sagittarius: 1995–2008 (13 years).

enter Aquarius in December and meet on December 21, 2020, at the 1st degree of Aquarius.

January 10, 2020 — Cancer Full Moon Lunar Eclipse and Cardinal Grand Cross

The emotional charge of the Saturn-Pluto conjunction is intensified by a lunar eclipse and grand cross two days before the January 12 conjunction (or basically at the same time).

The Cancer full Moon lunar eclipse forms a grand cross at 19-23 degrees of the cardinal signs (Aries, Cancer, Libra, and Capricorn).

Five planets (Pluto, Saturn, Jupiter, Sun, and Mercury), the asteroid Ceres, and the South Node are all in Capricorn. They form a grand cross with **Eris (mini planet) in Aries, Moon in Cancer, and asteroid Juno in Libra.** Mars in Sagittarius forms a semi-square with the Sun.

As explained in chapter 1, grand crosses are made up of squares and oppositions. This one is made more potent by the presence of five planets in Capricorn. Four (Sun, Pluto, Saturn, and Mercury) are conjunct (within 1 degree of each other). Jupiter is also in Capricorn.

As mentioned above, grand crosses happen between zodiac signs in one modality, with one or more planets in each of the four elements. The planets in this grand cross are in cardinal (active) signs (Aries, Cancer, Libra, and Capricorn).

As we will discuss later, the oppositions and squares indicate the high likelihood of conflict and tension. We are confronted with serious problems that we cannot ignore. The squares demand action and hard choices.

Juno in Libra

Juno represents the arena of relationships and intimacy, as well as the need for equality and freedom in relationships. In unconscious states, partners blame and project their needs and inner conflict on each other. Peace in partnership is possible only when both partners learn to consciously relate to the higher expression of both polarities and thus reconcile their own relationship with themselves, making it possible to stop projecting their inner turmoil on each other. Juno thus represents this spiritual self-regeneration that is necessary to achieve liberation in partnership.

When Juno is activated, and especially when Juno is in Libra, issues of intimacy, freedom, jealousy, insecurity, victimization, control trips, powerlessness, faith in oneself, and the ability to spiritually uplift oneself and to release old ways must be confronted and healed so that one may find fulfillment in committed relationships. Juno's ace strategy is to go into seclusion from time to time to re-center, renew, and spiritually rejuvenate.

Eris in Aries

Eris is a slow-moving dwarf planet with a 560-year cycle. Anyone born after 1937 has Eris in Aries. Currently, Eris is at 23 degrees Aries and will remain in Aries until June 2044.

Eris in Aries plays such an important role in the unfolding of consciousness in 2020 that I am writing another book devoted to this topic. To summarize here, Eris, the second-largest dwarf planet in the solar system, expresses the deep feminine, who is enraged by injustice and cries out until it is heard.

More specifically, Eris represents "the feminine principle of retributive justice"[6]; in other words, revenge looking for payback. In Greek mythology, Eris is known as the goddess of strife and discord, whose wrath is relentless. That doesn't sound like a story with a happy ending!

Eris was later viewed in the Christian tradition as a patron saint of chaotic creation. Consequently, the Eris archetype is chaos — the dynamic, yet unformed energy from which all creation is born. As chaos, Eris can also represent the freedom we have to create from the field of infinite possibilities. So Eris is not just a force of destruction, which is a natural part of the creation process, marking the end of one phase to make room for the next. This force continues to be active as it instills a dynamic power to move into the next phases of creativity.

Given this energetic makeup, Eris will form an "angry square" with the Capricorn group. Eris — as the mother of all — represents all parts of society that have been abused, left out, and exploited. Capricorn represents governmental and economic institutions, which are responsible for directly (through laws and policies) or indirectly (through greed, complicity, ignorance, or bad judgment) allowing structural violence and inequality to be institutionalized.

Eris thus symbolizes the dissatisfied masses who are waking up and speaking out. Social action threatens social cohesion when the grassroots populace is pitted against the institutions that it feels do not serve its interests but, on the contrary, ignore or work against them.

The United States' Pluto Return

The term *return* (Saturn return, Pluto return, Solar return, etc.) indicates that the transiting planet in the sky aligns with the exact placement of that planet in someone's (or something's) birth chart. The celestial body has completed its tour around the Sun and has returned to its original position.

It takes Pluto more than 240 years to cycle through the entire zodiac. (Humans would have to live to over 240 years to have a Pluto return. But we do experience our first Pluto square during our 30s and our Pluto opposition in our 80s.) Returns initiate new cycles by planting seeds that grow through the whole cycle. Noticeable events often appear around the actual date of the return, but the full effects take place over years. Long-range effects extend for many years, both before and after the exact date.

Using July 4, 1776, as the birth date of the United States, the U.S. Pluto return will happen on February 22, 2022, when Pluto is in 27 degrees Capricorn. Given the length of Pluto's cycle, we begin feeling its effects several years prior to the exact date. So we are already experiencing the dynamics of the end of a cycle and the beginning of something new.

---

[6] Ibid., 26.

The 2020 Saturn-Pluto alignment takes place near (within 4 degrees) Pluto in Capricorn in the birth chart of the United States. For a nation, Capricorn represents social, political, and governmental institutions and large corporations. The issues highlighted in the 2020 alignment are simply intensified in the U.S. Pluto return. They include (1) economic challenges; (2) civil unrest; (3) covert military engagements; (4) shocking scandals and the falling from grace of public individuals; (5) environmental problems dealing with food, poisons, land, and agriculture; and (6) autocratic power of the wealthy who consolidate their control.

Pluto digs up the past. America will need to contend with the legacy of slavery — racism, bigotry, and hatred. As explained by astrologer Ray Grasse, this includes attitudes toward immigration and minorities, "which seems rooted in a deeper fear or hatred of the 'other' and a disdain for all those who lie outside our familiar group or clan. One of Pluto's painful secrets seems to be just this: The hatred we direct toward others is actually *self*-hatred, but displaced outward."[7]

But becoming conscious of the fact that our attitudes are projections from our own psyche takes serious honesty, self-awareness, and courage. And herein lies the possibility or failure of Pluto's transformation and rebirth.

The U.S. Pluto return, like the 2020 conjunctions, presents us with both challenges and opportunities. The question is how we will deal with the issues that confront us. Can we survive the death/rebirth process, embrace healing, and be reborn into a more open and heart-centered society?

Previous Saturn-Pluto Conjunctions

Saturn-Pluto conjunctions occur about every 32–37 years. A Saturn-Pluto cycle lasts three-plus decades, 33–38 years. A look back at previous cycles indicates that significant events and trends are associated with each cycle.

1914 Saturn-Pluto Conjunction in Cancer

The Saturn-Pluto conjunction in 1914 coincided with the buildup to and outbreak of the first world war. This global conflict reshuffled the power dynamics in Europe by dissolving the Russian monarchy, the Ottoman Empire, and the Austro-Hungarian Empire, which led to the redrawing of national borders within Europe.

During the years 1921–1923, the Saturn square Pluto saw the emergence of fascism and totalitarianism in Europe (Mussolini and Stalin, followed by Hitler in the early 1930s). Another Saturn-Pluto square (1939–1941) occurred during World War II.

---

[7] Ray Grasse, "Turning Point: The United States' Pluto Return," *The Mountain Astrologer*, December 2019-January 2020, 26.

1947 Saturn-Pluto Conjunction in Leo

At the time of the conjunction in 1947, the German and Japanese empires had vanished, and the Cold War began. This cycle also saw the birth of the European Economic Union, created to loosen up market boundaries and expand trade between member countries.

The Saturn-Pluto conjunction in 1947 also saw the division between India and Pakistan and their establishment as individual nations. In the Middle East, Israel gained independence from the British in 1948.

At the end of this cycle (now), the vision of transcending cultural differences and nationalistic tendencies is seriously being challenged. Brexit (the UK exiting the European Union), several EU countries in or near bankruptcy, and serious populist threats to the usually stable political system in many countries around the issue of borders and refugees do not bode well for the EU's future.

1982 Saturn-Pluto Conjunction in Libra

The Saturn-Pluto cycle that began in 1982 marked a time of economic recession in the world, with the highest rate of unemployment in the U.S. since the Great Depression. It also marked the escalation of the Cold War during the Reagan years, later leading to the collapse of the Soviet bloc.

The Saturn-Pluto conjunction of 1982 coincided with the conservative policies of Ronald Regan in the U.S. and Thatcher in the United Kingdom (that is, the refinement of laissez-faire economic policies).

In the UK, Margaret Thatcher "freed" the markets by taking away the rules governing financial markets that had been created to avoid a reoccurrence of the Crash of 1929 and the Great Depression that followed. In the United States, Reaganomics did the same, allowing for the unrestrained power of financial institutions and corporations. The "greed machine" took advantage of deregulation, which resulted in the Savings and Loan crisis from 1986 to 1995, and culminated with the Great Recession that began in 2008.

Trickle-down economics became official policy and promoted the upward redistribution of wealth and increased income inequality. The top 10 percent got wealthier, and not much if anything trickled down to the lower 90 percent. By the mid-2010s, the combined wealth of the top 10 percent was nine times as much as the bottom 90 percent.

Saturn-Pluto in Capricorn: 1518 and 2020

1518: Martin Luther and the Protestant Reformation

The last Saturn-Pluto conjunction in Capricorn was in January 1518 — 502 years ago. Two months prior, Martin Luther, professor of moral theology at the University of Wittenberg,

Germany, nailed his 95 Theses to the All Saints' Church door in that city.

The Theses explained Luther's position against the practice of the Catholic clergy selling indulgences — certificates claiming to reduce punishment in purgatory for sins committed by the purchasers or their loved ones. Luther argued that the forgiveness of sins required inner spiritual repentance, for which a monetary purchase of an "indulgence" was not a valid substitute.

Luther's Theses were quickly reprinted, translated, and distributed throughout Germany and Europe. His challenges to papal authority initiated the Protestant Reformation. Luther was tried for heresy and excommunicated in 1521.

Comparing 1518 and 2020

The initiation of the Protestant Reformation highlights several Saturn-Pluto themes that are relevant in 2020. The Saturn-Pluto combination is about both the destruction and the empowerment (Pluto) of the establishment (Saturn). Capricorn is about social, political, and economic structures; hierarchical authority; government; and the use of institutionalized power. Pluto energies can act to undermine institutions that do not serve the common good and also be used to entrench the status quo. Both these forces seem to be currently active.

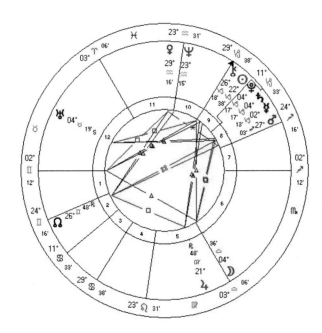

Saturn-Pluto Conjunction 1518
Jan. 3, 1518, 12:39 GMT
London, UK

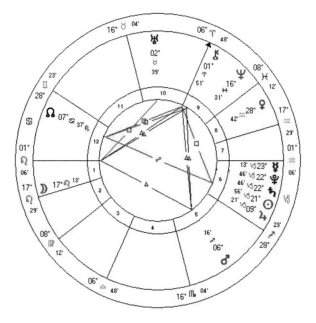

Saturn-Pluto Conjunction 2020
Jan. 12, 2020, 16:49 GMT
London, UK

More Details about the 1518 Alignment:

- Pluto and Saturn were conjunct at 4 degrees, and Mercury was close at 2 degrees. With Mercury involved, as it is in 2020, there was widespread discussion and dissemination of Luther's Theses, which initiated a pamphlet war. Attention in 2020 will of course be increased by the global reach of the Internet.
- Chiron was at 26 degrees Capricorn in 1518. The presence of Chiron, even though it was not closely aligned, added the theme of long-term impact and healing, definitely apt for the Protestant Reformation.

Seeds Are Planted

Regardless of the extent to which Pluto's deep messages succeed in getting attention, its inconvenient truths never go away. Accepted or not, seen or unseen, greater forces are always at work. Saturn-Pluto in Capricorn can further empower the current power structures. But this combination can also foment a revolution against them. This was what Martin Luther did to the Catholic Church. His actions seeded a revolution that couldn't be stopped. Pluto plants seeds that grow and grow.

The 1518 precedent of the successful opposition to the entrenched establishment (the Catholic Church) could be relevant in 2020, as seeds may be planted for an eventual successful movement against power structures, including governments and multinational corporations whose basic interest is enriching themselves at the expense of the rest of the global population.

The 2020 Saturn-Pluto conjunction is thus likely to both embolden those of power and wealth and motivate others to purse active resistance against it.

How Cycles Play Out

How a given cycle will play out is usually not understood until its last quarter. In other words, we can't accurately predict what is going to happen and will only know after it happens.

For example, the long-term implications of policies initiated at the beginning of the current (now ending) 1982 Saturn-Pluto conjunction in Libra became clear only in 2011 when the Occupy Movement (young people protesting on Wall Street just after the waning, last square, of the cycle) brought widespread awareness to serious income disparities in the United States.

We have the next 2020 Saturn-Pluto cycle to witness the effects of the tax bill passed by the U.S. Congress in December 2017, giving tax breaks to the rich. It is not looking too good for anyone but the wealthy so far.

The 2020 Jupiter-Pluto Cycle: Spring 2020

Jupiter and Pluto meet every 12.5 years. The last time they met was in 2007 in Sagittarius.

These two planets conjunct in Capricorn three times in 2020 — early April, late June, and mid-November. Because they are within 4–6 degrees of each other, their interaction and the effects they precipitate are ongoing from the beginning of March 2020 until Jupiter moves into Aquarius in December 2020.

The exact dates are
March 29–April 5: Jupiter and Pluto in 24 degrees Capricorn
June 22–30: Jupiter and Pluto in 24 degrees Capricorn (Jupiter is retrograde)
November 7–13: Jupiter and Pluto in 22 degrees Capricorn

The Forces of Greed

For those operating from a position of greed, the Jupiter-Pluto pair can further fuel a "might makes right" attitude. In Capricorn, expansionistic ambitions of the "greed machine" are fueled, power grabs and mega-ambitions of those in power are rationalized, and exploitation of the ignorant and vulnerable are pursued with more and more vigor.

Jupiter interjects at least a discussion of ethical considerations. However, those with economic power generally distance themselves from these "irrelevant" topics. In a world where survival of the fittest is a justified norm, it is easy to not only remain aloof, but to believe that one's operational paradigm is an unquestionable truth. Supply and demand economics can justify anything that it wants to. Jupiter's principles are superseded by profitability.

Under the influence of the 2020 Jupiter-Pluto cycle, it is easy to see how the excesses of the wealthy and expansion (Jupiter) of power (Pluto) can bring about further consolidation of the economic and political status quo through globalization and massive acquisitions. Destabilization would then increase as inflation, monopolies, and deregulation stimulate unsustainable growth and fortify the coffers of the already very wealthy. Income inequality within and between nations would become more and more apparent, and untenable at the individual level.

The Good News

The good news is that the Jupiter-Pluto cycle points to all of the above being exposed. The greed machine may reach its zenith, but at least it will be common knowledge that the system is designed to consolidate wealth for a few while disregarding the impact of exploitative norms on the masses. Awareness of what is happening can motivate other segments of the population to step forward, offer alternatives, and work to create systems that serve the common good.

The other good news is that those who choose to engage in their own healing and honestly deal with their negative and self-sabotaging programming can elevate themselves into the light of consciousness. It may be a heavy path to tread for a while, but the rewards are great when we remember that Pluto's goal is to awaken us to higher love.

The Aquarius Jupiter-Saturn Cycle: Dec. 21, 2020

Jupiter and Saturn conjunctions occur every 20 years. Libra initiated a new cycle in 1980, and Taurus in 2000.

Jupiter enters Aquarius and meets with Saturn at the 1st degree of Aquarius right at the 2020 winter solstice, initiating a new 20-year Jupiter-Saturn cycle. The rendezvous of the two planets of "social destiny" (Jupiter and Saturn) is preceded by a total solar eclipse on December 14, initiating a paradigm shift in the social area — education, religion, culture, and the arts.

The necessity for change is thus supported by the opportunities to create new social and economic structures, ways of being, and attitudes that help create needed fundamental changes in the next two decades.

This conjunction at the 1st degree of Aquarius starts a 200-year-long series of Jupiter-Saturn cycles in the air signs (see below).[8] This is a key marker for the Aquarian Age.

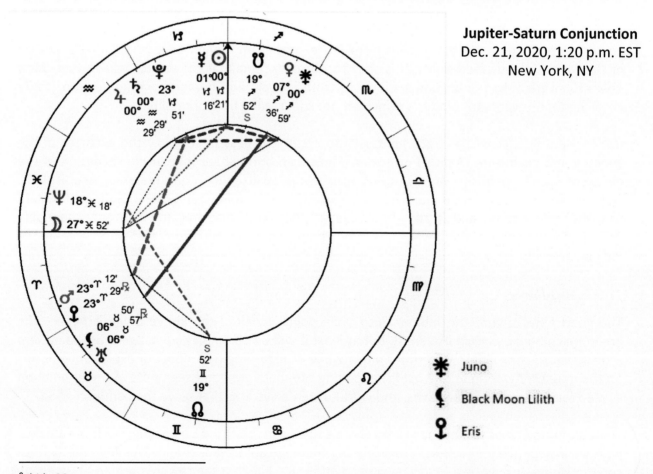

Jupiter-Saturn Conjunction
Dec. 21, 2020, 1:20 p.m. EST
New York, NY

---

[8] Ibid., 29.

An Uncomfortable Chart

This is not a comforting or comfortable chart, as it also contains explosive elements. Mars (the warrior) and Eris (perpetually angry) join up (conjunct) in Aries. This volatile pair squares Pluto. The big question is, How do we use or upgrade this fire energy to shift out of being a destructive force into constructive creation? The answer is yet unknown. Egotistical Mars is aggressive. Vengeful Eris wants payback. Egotistical, emotionally immature Aries energy has a short fuse and doesn't think things out before it acts. It doesn't ask first, "How will this end?"

Negative Possibilities

Projected through the group mind via the Internet, volatile and unrestrained emotions can direct mass consciousness in very negative ways. The energy is inflammatory and can feed the anger of those seeking revenge and retribution and of those who feel frustrated, left out, exploited, unheard, and powerless.

Those in power can use the volatile situation to legitimize more power grabs and consolidation of power. This energy can be directed toward inciting more gun violence, militarism, reactionary populism, and war mongering.

The energies can also cause us to look more carefully at the above aspects of our current reality and take steps to shift our passion from the irrational to more meaningful and useful ways of dealing with what is going on. Probably both will happen.

Positive Possibilities

The saving grace will be our ability to direct the passion of fire energy toward creating more just, respectful, and equitable institutions. The nature of the global collective consciousness (composed of individual consciousnesses) will determine how we use the energy of this conjunction in the next 20 years.

The defining question is, To what extent can more and more people transcend their primitive egoistic tendencies and choose love over anger and fear? The bottom line is each of us are at choice. We can each do our part by choosing how we navigate our personal lives and how we participate in collective endeavors. We can impact the global collective by shifting from angry aggressiveness to courageous action, truth telling, and compassion for all.

Either way — in destruction or creative transformation — this energy is unstoppable. We can influence the course of history by interacting and serving with compassion and love.

Whether we realize it at the time or later, the conjunction of Saturn and Jupiter at the 1st degree of Aquarius is a major marker thrusting us into the Aquarian Age.

Jupiter-Saturn Cycles Shift from the Earth to Air Signs

Jupiter and Saturn initiate a new social cycle every 20 years, which sets the tone for shifts in cultural attitudes and social patterns.

Jupiter and Saturn in the Earth Signs
The Jupiter-Saturn conjunction in Capricorn in 1842 initiated the earth element series at the beginning of the Industrial Revolution.[9]

For the last 178 years, the 20-year Jupiter-Saturn cycles happened in the earth signs. This period of modernity and industrialization witnessed the growth of heavy industry and earth-derived energy sources, or fossil fuels. Wealth, materialism, and upgrading the standard of living with innumerable inventions and creature comforts "consumed" our attention. Physical reality, or the realm of matter, was more important and got more attention than the mind and spirit.

The last Jupiter-Saturn cycle, which began on May 28, 2000, at 23 degrees Taurus, focused our attention and concerns on the economy and business. Greed was the touchstone that led to the global financial crisis that began in 2008.

New Cycles in the Air Signs
The new 180-year series of Jupiter-Saturn cycles in the air signs begins in 2020. Focusing on the mental and spiritual realm is new territory.

Aquarius Sets the Tone for the Future

Aquarius represents the cool, detached, intellectual quest for the truth and its application in human society. Ideally, the Water Bearer, who downloads consciousness into the higher mind, will help modulate the current emotionally and ideologically driven polarization. A neutral, nonjudgmental force is needed to calm the overexaggerated and distorted attitudes fueled by prejudice, fabricated facts, and irrational thought.

The air element espouses objective facts, hard data, and objective observation. A global nonpersonal perspective transcends personal preferences, which are often fueled by intense emotions and attachment to one's ideological opinion.

Aquarius thinks in scientific ways and examines humanity's role in both creating and finding solutions to global crises. Future-oriented, Aquarius not only accommodates the new, it is the instigator of revolutionary thought and action. Aquarius works for the community and global identities that transcend socioeconomic, ethnic, racial, and nationalistic classifications.

Aquarius knows that humanity must work together as a team. Aquarius strives to be fair to all those involved — all humanity. For Aquarius and the Aquarian Age, each individual is a unique, important, and irreplaceable part of the human family.

Pluto in Aquarius in 2023

The Saturn-Jupiter conjunction in December 2020 initiates a new Aquarian cycle. Pluto joins in when it enters Aquarius in 2023. The last time Pluto was in Aquarius, in the late 1700s, saw the first wave of mechanization and the Industrial Revolution.

Aquarius is the sign of surprises, rebellion, and revolution. Pluto seeds and seeks renewal and structural transformation. With Pluto in Aquarius, we can expect deep-seated changes stemming from innovative breakthroughs in many areas of life. Technological advances can greatly improve the quality of life, but they can also be disruptive.

For example, the massive use of robots will dramatically increase unemployment, excluding much of the human population from a means to make a viable living, and further support an economic system owned and run by a privileged few. Less or no job security for the general population and rising inequality will destabilize society and foment protests and action for fundamental change.

> ***Aquarius knows that humanity must work together as a team.*** Aquarius strives to be fair to all those involved — all humanity. For Aquarius and the Aquarian Age, each individual is a unique, important, and irreplaceable part of the human family.

---

[9] Ibid., 30.

Chapter 4:
A Deeper Look at the 2020 Alignments

There are many different opinions about and ways to analyze the 2020 alignments — what they mean and how they will play out. In this section we share and synthesize different perspectives.

Keywords

The effects of the planetary cycles involving Pluto, Uranus, and Saturn penetrate into the core of our human challenges. The tone and themes for the 2020s set out by Saturn and Pluto are neither comfortable nor easygoing. Keywords include *extreme*, *transformative*, *serious*, and potentially both *destructive* and *creative*.[10]

What Pluto Is About

Pluto is about transformative power, how and why power is acquired and lost. Pluto reshapes both our inner and outer realities — our psyche, our society, and its systems.

Pluto represents how we personally and collectively express and are affected by raw, primal power. The transformative shifts demanded by Pluto have a profound impact on our psyche and our society — both explosive (like a volcanic eruption) and implosive (as in a meltdown of a nuclear reactor).

A transpersonal planet, Pluto and its workings are hidden from our conscious view and are often inexplicable and uncontrollable. Yet we cannot avoid the intrusive and sweeping effects on all aspects of human life.[11]

What Saturn Is About

Saturn is about holding physical reality together through the establishment and maintenance of order and stable structures. Saturn usually resists change and can be conservative and reactionary.

Saturn deals with the practical side of physical reality that we can see, measure, and perceive consciously. Its domain is both our personal authority and the power and position of the social authorities of our collective institutions.

Alone and together, we face problems to solve and challenges to overcome. Our task is to find solutions and to empower ourselves by effectively dealing with our life situations. Saturn is

---

[10] Bill Herbst, "The 2020 Jupiter-Saturn-Pluto Alignments," *The Mountain Astrologer*, December 2018-January 2019, 33–37.
[11] Ibid., 33.

about creating our life over our lifetime and achieving individual mastery in the process.

Collectively, Saturn is about building social, economic, and political structures that deal with common issues and interests, including government, education, and healthcare.

Saturn and the Outer Planets

Saturn is the manifester in our personal world. Saturn is about bringing ideas into form. Combined with the energy of an outer planet, many things can happen.

Outer planets are not visible to the naked eye and operate at an unconscious level. They definitely affect us, but it is hard to figure out how to identify and deal with their subtle influences.

Saturn orbits between the inner and outer planets — one foot in the physical world and one foot in the outer dimensions of reality. Add Saturn to Uranus, Neptune, or Pluto and Saturn can serve as a transmitter of their energies onto the physical plane. Saturn is a bridge between the inner and outer planets, between our personal identity and our fate or destiny.

When Saturn links up with an outer planet, it serves as a channel for its energies to create tangible effects in the world. For example, when Saturn conjuncted Uranus-Neptune at the end of 1989, the Berlin Wall came down. In 2001, when Saturn opposed Pluto, 9/11 happened.

The Impact

The impacts of the meeting of the powerful forces represented by Saturn and Pluto involve

- ♦ The redistribution of power in the world and who will make decisions that affect the collective
- ♦ Both obvious and hidden power plays to take and maintain power
- ♦ Who and what mindset or paradigm will be in power positions that determine how we use collective resources

How this cycle plays out will be determined by the integrity and morality of those in authority. Who (if anyone) will have the capacity and resilience to manage power in a way that fairly distributes power and resources?

Initial Effects

Initially, a new Saturn-Pluto cycle is highlighted by a reaction and challenge to the status quo. This challenge is met with resistance by those who try to maintain and consolidate the power and control of the existing power structure.[12]

A stellium in Capricorn, including the Sun, Mercury, Saturn, Pluto, and Ceres, all squaring Eris is

---

[12] Ibid.

highly significant.

In world events, Saturn conjunct Pluto in Capricorn represents large organizations like multinational corporations; superpower countries; the UN, NATO, and WHO; and trading blocs like the European Union.

Uranus-Pluto

Many deeper underlying trends have been exposed by the interaction of Uranus and Pluto since 2000, during which time many "secrets" have been revealed.

Together Uranus and Pluto have stirred the bottom of the pot, tore apart the illusion of stability, and replaced complacency with insecurity. The once hidden secrets that were exposed, and are still surfacing, provide the fodder to support major challenges to our collective institutions.

The interaction of Uranus and Pluto gets our attention and wakes us up to what we have been ignoring. Once brought to our attention, we can no longer ignore the elephants in the room. This is a revolutionary cycle because it sets in motion new agendas for dealing with heretofore obscured, ignored, or silently denied problems. The status quo is challenged, and this challenge, once revealed, will not go away until we deal with it. The conjunctions in 2020 impel us to deal with the multiple elephants in many rooms.

Signs of the Breakdown of Collective Institutions

The involvement of Pluto with other planets can breed extremism, polarization, bloodshed, and other symptoms of systemic breakdown. Factions demonize each other, justify their ideological positions, and use (and make up) different facts to tenaciously support their opinions and beliefs.[13]

The discounting of long-standing norms of civility, free speech, civil rights, and justice not only threatens social cohesiveness and political stability, the loss and weakening of collective values erode the underpinnings of society. Trouble is brewing when the public no longer trusts its basic institutions and when the "leaders" are co-opted by self-interest.

Hard Times

The negative effects of Saturn-Pluto interactions are associated with the worst abuses of power and corruption, including organized criminality and mass shootings. Conjunctions, squares, and oppositions involving Saturn and Pluto often coincide with unfortunate and disruptive occurrences, such as the beginning of World War II and 9/11.

This Saturn-Pluto conjunction could bring about the demise of important economic, corporate,

---

[13] Ibid., 27.

and political power structures and the downfall and disgrace of those who occupy positions of power in those institutions. Debt-burdened major corporations, governments, banks, and other economic institutions could come to a grinding halt, signifying the death of the old, established political-economic power structure. These power structures could become even more oppressive and tyrannical as they desperately try to remain in control.

There can be hard times for many segments of the global population when these two serious planets align.

The Reality of Globalization

The Saturn-Pluto cycle can also initiate shifts in geopolitical dynamics affecting the distribution of global power.

Globalization has resulted in the consolidation of wealth at the top the shifting of economic power from the West to the East, unsustainable national debts, and the inability to identify who really is in charge. Globalization has empowered multinational corporations, who are becoming more powerful than national governments. When corporations are the controlling economic and political force in the world, national governments become even less effective at promoting the greater good for all of its citizens.

The Upheaval of Automation

The Aquarian Age is optimally about working together as a global family. Technological innovations are also a major theme of Aquarius. After a new Saturn-Jupiter cycle at the 1st degree of Aquarius is launched in December 2020, social issues related to the negative effects of technology are going to give rise to more public concern. The effects of mass automation are one example.

As a result of automation, up to 47 percent of both white- and blue-collar jobs in developed countries will disappear by 2045, according to a recent study by Oxford University. No country seriously acknowledges or is preparing to deal with the massive loss of jobs that intensive automation will create.[14]

In the past (decades ago), increased productivity and profit raised the standard of living for workers. But no more! Automation increases productivity, but the increased profits are currently destined to go into the pockets of investors and executives, leaving out and impoverishing millions. Automated technologies are not designed to help workers or make their work safer. Their purpose is to eliminate workers, squeeze more out of who is left, and enrich corporations and their executives.

Amazon's high-tech warehouses are an example of the squeeze. The workers who are left are heavily monitored, with warnings and even terminations when their productivity is not considered adequate. The median wage of Amazon warehouse workers is about $28,500 a

---

[14] See Ramesh Srinivasan, "Opinion: Automation Is Likely to Eliminate Nearly Half Our Jobs in the Next 25 Years. Here's What to Do," *Los Angeles Times*, October 30, 2019.

year. CEO Jeff Bezos earns about $9 million an hour!

The future tidal wave of automation will significantly expand the current economic inequities. Already, in the United States, "the top one-tenth of 1% of the population earns nearly as much as the bottom 90% of the population combined."[15]

Creative solutions and a shift in attitude toward serving, not exploiting, people are necessary. Less greed and more compassion could certainly help.

Challenges and Opportunities

When Mars retrogrades in Aries and squares the Saturn-Pluto conjunction (later in 2020), serious political and social conflicts could heat up.

Major discontent can surface when more and more of the world's population understands that the "new world order" is not supportive of, and is in fact working against, their interests and needs. This realization can bring more demands from the grassroots for structural change.

The egregious disparity in wealth, power, and privilege can become unbearable for those who live in disturbing financial hardship. More segments of the population may rebel against systems that no longer (or never did) support them.

Feeling restricted and limited can also motivate us to change both our inner and outer environments. Pluto and Saturn can empower us to support ourselves and each other in working toward financial freedom and prosperity, becoming both successful entrepreneurs and active participants in collective life.

Saturn and Pluto Spell Crisis

Together Saturn-Pluto can precipitate a crisis stemming from no longer viable collective institutions that do not meet the needs of all segments of the collective. The need for fundamental changes in our collective systems and the challenges have their deep roots in untenable restrictions on our freedom and well-being.

The Dynamics of Power

Power is the underlying dynamic in the Saturn-Pluto pairing. Power can be used destructively or constructively. Both are likely and depend on our personal and collective choices.

The negative, or lower-consciousness, uses of Saturn-Pluto energies are not pretty. The power ignited by Saturn-Pluto can entail coercive force by authorities. Angry, revengeful, and defensive impulses can fuel repressive and destructive actions.

---

[15] Ibid.

Polarization Is the Norm
Under the Pluto-Saturn influence, each side tends to see themselves threatened by the other — the enemy. Perceptions of reality are formed by black-and-white thinking and absolute ideologies. Polarization becomes the norm. When the human population chooses to identify with extremes, with no room for differences of opinion and acceptable diversity, conflict ensues. When our mind is conflicted, we play the conflict out in visible physical reality. When there is no give and take and no listening to the other, disagreements cannot be resolved as compromise and cooperation are no longer possible.

Many Options
There is a wide range of options for how the energies of astrological archetypes express. Basically, it depends upon or is predominately influenced by

1. Individual and collective consciousness
2. The current state of collective institutions
3. The belief system or ideology that directs social institutions
4. Those in power and how they choose to use their positions of power

The Upside and Gifts

When the constructive use of power is backed up by moral, emotional, and spiritual fortitude, we tap into the gifts of Saturn and Pluto. However, we must be able to dig deep enough to find and claim them. These intense energies can offer us the inner conviction and strength to persevere during times of extreme hardship and in situations where the odds appear to be heavily stacked against us. We find we are able to stand up to seemingly insurmountable problems with optimistic determination and belief in a power greater than human greed — the heart!

The positive potential of the Saturn-Pluto collaboration is linked to honestly confronting its negative manifestations. The courage to recognize deep causes and to take responsibility in the face of the difficulties involved make it possible to direct and sustain the determined efforts required to work toward authentic change. Not only results, but deep wisdom and satisfaction, are born from the experience of confronting suffering from the heart.

The upside is the dawning realization of those who understand that they cannot passively sit back and trust that things will turn out okay. When enough people realize that things are not going to change without their participation and start taking responsibility for their lives and the part that they can play in upgrading our society, an unstoppable collective force is ignited.

A Challenging Crossroads

We are at a challenging crossroads. Extreme polarization that divides how we view reality into us and enemies dominated by fear and anger does not bode well for a more inclusive, compassionate, and kind outcome.

We need hope, and our attitude is critical. But wishful thinking is not enough. We can glean optimism from the fact that reality may force us to give up our cherished illusions and constructively work toward practical solutions to common problems that affect us all, such as climate change, gun violence, the opioid crisis, homelessness and poverty, endless wars creating displaced populations, access to affordable health care, equitable educational and justice systems, and corruption in politics.

Hope and optimism come from the ability to operate from inner peace, a desire for social harmony and well-being for all, and the ability to transcend ideologies and operate from the heart. *Tenacity*, *courage*, and *trust* are the keywords.

We Gain Strength and Heart Power Through Perseverance

In addition to the challenges, we are being supported and given the strength to persevere during times of extreme hardship and in situations where the odds appear to be heavily stacked against us. We find we are able to stand up to seemingly insurmountable problems with optimistic determination and belief in a power greater than human greed — the heart!

Chapter 5:
Where Are the Other Planets in 2020?

The study of astrology is about translating the symbolism of the zodiac signs and the planets into the psychological, emotional, mental, and physical aspects of our human experience. All the planets and their current zodiac energies play a role in the overall picture. Below we discuss the other planets and how they impact the 2020 period of transformation.

Neptune in Pisces

Dates: Neptune transits through Pisces from April 5, 2011, to March 30, 2025.

Neptune is the (ruler) zodiac sign associated with Pisces. Pisces is the third and last water sign. As part of the water trio (with Cancer and Scorpio), Pisces deals with the emotions. Pisces and Neptune are discussed in relationship to the twelfth house in chapter 11.

Neptune transits can create confusion, uncertainty, and breakdowns, which can be dealt with only by connecting to, trusting, and surrendering to a higher power. Ultimately, Neptune can lead us out of illusionary pursuits into the reality of divine love.

For those who wish to check the possible interaction of transiting Neptune in their birth chart, Neptune will be at 16 degrees Pisces at the Pluto-Saturn conjunction on January 12, moving through 19–20 degrees Pisces during the Pluto-Jupiter conjunctions, and back at 18 degrees Pisces (after a period of retrograde) at the Saturn-Jupiter conjunction in December.

Issues Related to Neptune in Pisces

Some of the issues that have moved to the forefront since Neptune entered Pisces include the following:

- Water-related crises featuring drought, rising sea levels, and flooding
- Mental and emotional health
- Drugs and addiction — the overprescribing and overuse of opioids and antidepressants
- Anxiety and stress from general uncertainty, poverty, and all areas of overwhelm
- Blurring of the line between fact and fiction, the truth and lies

Neptune in Pisces also encourages us to reevaluate our use of technology, recognize how science and spirituality cohabit the same reality, and witness our oneness with nature.

Uranus in Taurus

Dates: March 5, 2019 – July 6, 2025

Date details: May 16, 2018 – November 6, 2018, and March 5, 2019 – July 6, 2025
(Retrograde Uranus moved back into Aries for four months between November 7, 2018, and March 4, 2019.)

Linked Up to the Universal Mind

Uranus is the higher octave of Mercury. Mercury symbolizes the mind, reasoning, discriminating, analyzing, and knowledge-seeking. Uranus symbolizes a conscious intellect that has transcended prejudice, beliefs, and ideology. With Uranus, the mind awakens to a new level of seeking and knowledge. Uranus links our mind to the universal mind.

Under Uranus influence, a force beckons us to discover what is yet undiscovered. Uranus is a seeker of wisdom and truth, knowing that nothing is final or definitive. Under its influence, we are driven to explore an expanded experience of life and new ways of self-expression.

When we become responsive to the intuitive knowing of the higher mind, we can feel what is right for us and we trust our intuition to guide us.

Surprises and the Unexpected

Uranus in Taurus can precipitate natural disasters and seismic and volcanic activity. Days before Uranus entered Taurus, the Kilauea volcano erupted in Hawaii, lasting for months and creating great destruction on the Big Island.

Taurus reminds us of the good things in life that bring us pleasure and comfort. Uranus reminds us that they can all be taken away if we pursue a lifestyle that is too extravagant for our budget. How can we go into the future on a sound financial footing? Maybe there are other earning opportunities that we need to explore, which are directed by our mission to serve.

With Uranus in Taurus, and the North Node in Cancer (see below), health is a major concern. Taking care of our body, which includes aspects of our lifestyle, gets top billing. This may include becoming more aware of food addictions, toxins in our diets, and inflammation of our gut as primary sources of chronic disease. A corresponding greater awareness of the importance of our microbiome may lead to a revolution in personalized health care.

Uranus is always ready to deliver wakeup calls. Taurus reminds us to pay attention to how we feel so we become aware without needing catastrophes. We get hints every day in life.

North Node in Cancer and South Node in Capricorn

Dates: November 2018 – May 2020

Date details: The South Node is in Capricorn and the North Node is in Cancer from November 7, 2018, through May 30, 2020. North Node will then be in Gemini and the South Node in Sagittarius from May 5, 2020, to January 30, 2022. (The nodes travel in reverse order through the zodiac.)

Definition

The symbol of the ascending North Node is ☊, and the symbol of the descending South Node is ☋. In Vedic astrology, the North Node is called Rahu and the South Node is Ketu. The nodes operate in pairs and remain in opposite, or complementary, signs for about one and a half years.

The two lunar nodes are points in the sky, not planets, which are determined by the time when the Moon crosses the ecliptic, or apparent path, of the Sun in the sky. The *ascending* North Node is where the Moon moves into the northern ecliptic hemisphere, while the *descending* South Node is where the Moon enters the southern ecliptic hemisphere.

In astrology, the North and South Nodes represent cosmic directives that instruct us about what must be healed from the past to move into the future. The nodes in Capricorn and Cancer add an important dynamic to the 2020 alignments in Capricorn, which feature the qualities, tests, challenges, and mission of the Capricorn archetype discussed below.

South Node in Capricorn

The South Node represents our past and what we must deal with to move on. The South Node also represents the soul qualities that we have developed in past lives and must bring to the fore to move into the future and deal with new territory. Capricorn qualities include courage, perseverance, grit, and patience.

The Capricorn archetype represents our personal journey, who we are in the world and our lifelong climb up our own mountain. South Node in Capricorn lessons are about letting go of superficial and social expressions of recognition related to attaining prestige, success, and honor in the world. What is important is how we judge ourselves, how true we are to our own values, and how judiciously we use our personal resources.

Our Tests Are Significant
We are tested, and our tests have deep significance for our soul and its journey to self-realization. The Capricorn mountain goat climbs alone with patience and persistence. At each moment and each stage, we must calculate the risks. Benefits come only if we calculate well and are able to continue on our journey. Nothing stops us from pursuing our quest. We must obtain our objectives, which can be the highest of human aspirations or the lowest abuses of power. The question is how we use our strength and for what purpose.

How We Use Our Resources
Money and material possessions to enjoy a good life are important to Capricorn. But we must be vigilant to avoid needing to impress others and gaining positions of power at the expense of our own health, well-being, and integrity.

We must constantly evaluate how we use our inner and physical resources. Effectiveness and efficiency are key factors. But are we working to serve our own interests or are we committed to serving the higher good of humanity?

Authority and Mission
Ultimately, Capricorn's authority is delegated and defined by our soul. It is our mission and our destiny to do what we came here to do. We gain deep and lasting satisfaction only when our life is on purpose. Awakened or conscious Capricorn leads with humility. With less maturity, false pride and self-importance become two rocks that can trip us and send us falling down the mountain.

Capricorn must earn its rewards and respect. Wealth and power come with responsibility.

Immature Capricorn can feel inadequate. The goat overcomes obstacles through the necessity of dealing with life's challenges, the determination to achieve its goals, and a commitment to finding purpose in life. It persists relentlessly as it climbs the mountain. Capricorn has to learn to be flexible and flowing to get to high places and stay there.

Positive Qualities
It is wise to take advantage of all this Capricorn energy and its positive qualities — persistence, patience, practicality, efficiency, ambition, and willingness to work hard for what we want. In its strength, Capricorn is dependable, confident, and gives others confidence as well.

The Realm of Higher Love
Ultimately our head and heart must unite. The goat becomes a unicorn with its awakening of the third eye to truth and knowledge. This is the goal of the path of self-initiation. Through struggle and right use of power, one is initiated into the realm of higher love.

North Node in Cancer

The North Node in Cancer draws our attention to our inner-emotional reality and emphasizes the importance of learning to operate from inner caring, nurturing, and self-love.

The Deep Feminine
The Cancer archetype is the most feminine and represents the nurturing and unconditional love of the Mother. The North Node in Cancer stimulates the awakening of the empowered feminine, which is new territory for the planet, for women, and for men. Connecting with, honoring, and healing our emotional body are basic to embracing the empowered feminine.

Cancer — Emotional Enmeshment

The North Node in Cancer reminds us that it is the human condition to be emotionally connected to others. We start our human journey being completely emotionally attached and one with our mother. As we grow up, we become emotionally enmeshed with other human beings, usually with siblings, other family members, and then with friends and sexual partners.

The North Node in Cancer focuses our growth process on releasing unhealthy emotional attachments by disengaging from others' stories, opinions about us, expectations, and demands. This emotional detachment is absolutely necessary to connect with ourselves, our soul, and the divine, and to be able to use our energy for our own life and our own creations.

In the Capricorn climb up the mountain of life, enmeshment prevents us from reaching our own peak. We can't ascend if we are carrying emotional baggage that we acquired by imposed and chosen emotional attachments.

The Cancer archetype and the fourth house are about creating a safe and separate reality within ourselves as the foundation from which we are able to separate, create our own autonomy, and be self-supportive, self-nurturing, and self-reliant.

From Past to Present and Future

In sum, the current position of the nodes in Cancer/Capricorn are about stepping out of a repressed and dysfunctional emotional past so we can create our future less encumbered by inner-child emotional wounds and programming. We can make peace with and learn from the past. Recognizing how perspectives form our interpretations, we can reinterpret events to heal wounded feelings and any sense of victimhood.

We can notice when we operate from past perspectives or conditioning. And we can train ourselves to be emotionally aware in the present and make more conscious choices about how we act and react. In present feeling awareness, we open up to the possibility of no longer being controlled by things that we once considered an annoyance or a threat to our tranquility and security.

Chiron in Aries

Dates: February 2019 – June 2026

Date details: Chiron first entered Aries on April 17, 2018, and then retrograded into Pisces on September 25, 2018. On February 18, 2019, Chiron re-entered Aries, where it remains until June 19, 2026. Our healing journey for these next eight years focuses on establishing our personal soul identity and our mission this lifetime.[16]

---

[16] Chiron's last journey through Aries (1968—1977) included the mass peace demonstrations against the Vietnam War, the assassinations of Martin Luther King Jr. and Robert Kennedy, and the impeachment of Nixon.

In Greek mythology, Chiron was the centaur known for his wise healing solutions for wounded heroes. Chiron represents the integration and inseparability of our humanness and the sacred. A basic Chiron theme is that it is through our personal healing that we prepare ourselves to offer our special gifts of healing wisdom to others.

The Chiron archetype helps us identify and work on where we perceive ourselves to be weak and not good enough. We heal ourselves by identifying and upholding our values and taking charge of our life based on our own definition and destiny.

Chiron Healing and Empowerment

In Aries, Chiron turns our attention toward investigating the warrior/hero aspect of self-healing. With Chiron in Aries, our healing happens as we find and empower our soul and its innate qualities. We have to be brave enough to get in touch with and acknowledge how fear and anger have controlled our inner reality. Then we have to give up focusing on the fear and anger and use these energies to be honest with ourselves about what we really want and need. When honesty replaces shame, guilt, and judgment, we find inner freedom and authenticity. Our primal energies become available for living. Instead of repressing our feelings and power and recoiling from life, we awaken to the aliveness of being.

Ultimately, Chiron in Aries opens the door to reclaiming our personal power. Spiritual warriors act from love, not fear. We stand in sacred space; we honor and protect the sacredness of all life. Our journey to the sacred realm happens through acceptance, compassion, kindness, and forgiveness.

Healing happens when we are able to face our fears, dissolve old patterns, and see who we really are — a child of the Universe, no more and no less deserving than anyone else. Where Chiron is located in our birth chart is where we must develop the inner, spiritual qualities of that sign and house. While transiting in Aries, Chiron focuses our attention on where we hesitate to fully shine our light. *How do we distract ourselves or stay busy to avoid our feelings? Where do we need to take a stand, a risk, a chance?*

Chiron and Eris

Dates: Chiron moved into Aries on April 17, 2018, and catches up to Eris at 25 degrees in May 2025.

Chiron and Eris both in Aries highlight where open wounds remain around masculine energy and willpower. Chiron in Aries signifies a wounding around confidence, self-esteem, and identity; a sense of defeatism, where we don't feel we have the right to ask or have what we want, or that it's okay to be our true self. The more we have committed to our own healing work, the better prepared we are to mentor and guide others.

Our experience of our authentic self is possible only when the healed expressions of both polarities (stable mind and flowing emotions) are awakened in both men and women. Both the feminine and the masculine have been seriously wounded, resulting in an inner war. The wounding happened because both polarities have been misunderstood and misused.

Mars in Aries for Six Months

Dates: June 28, 2020 – January 6, 2021

Mars is in Aries for six months, seeding emotionally irritable conditions. We can feel both agitated and energized.

During the time Mars is in Aries (from June 28, 2020, to January 6, 2021), Mars will be retrograde from September 10 to November 13. During retrogrades, we are well advised to lie low, wait for divine timing, and be patient with how events evolve. It is best to trust that we will receive rewards due from past efforts.

It is also important to not overtax our physical body and nervous system by trying to do too much to push forward. Mars retrograde is a good time to do inner-healing work, especially related to inner anger and resentments. It's also advisable to avoid any tendencies to compete that can prevent cooperation and seed conflict.

It is worth pointing out that Mars will be retrograde in Aries during the U.S. presidential election in early November 2020.

Be the Author of Your Own Life

Ultimately Aries is about being authentically ourselves. Authentic comes from the root word *author*. Chiron, Eris, and Mars in Aries all encourage us to be authors of our own lives.

Chapter 6:
Your Soul Path Astrology for 2020 and Beyond

Personal — How Will All This Play Out?

"So how will this all play out in my life?" That is a very good question! Each of us will be affected in our own special way. To use this transformational energy constructively, it is important to see our personal life from the evolutionary perspective of moving out of the grip of fear into the heart space of love.

Saturn-Pluto Transits Are Heavy

Many of us will ask, "Why do I feel this way?"

With both Saturn and Pluto aligned, we are very likely to feel burdened by heavy fear-based feelings, confusing emotions, and negative thoughts that don't feel like love. Some will feel discouraged, disappointed, depressed, even hopeless. Some will feel lost and not know what to do. Even if we remain optimistic, Saturn may slow us down.

All of the above and more are part of the evolutionary process. If we stick with it, we will make it through. The best part of Saturn and Pluto transits is when they are over! There is always some form of gold that we can mine when we dig deep enough into the richness of our life and our soul.

What Can We Do?

When we feel uncertain, we can ask for clarity and wait until we feel guided to take action.

We can't know how things are going to play out until we move in one direction or another. When we feel ready, we can take one careful step at a time, but we must take a step!

It is natural to try to seek security. Some will seek security by reverting to the past and traditional ways of doing things. However, the only "secure" solution for existential anguish is to connect with and trust a higher power and our soul.

Much is going on that we can't see. Information is encoded in all our life experiences. We shouldn't discount, minimize, or try to avoid our own life challenges. We must identify them and deal with them. This is how we cultivate our power, build inner strength and self-esteem, and find out what is really happening.

The Universe speaks to us in so many ways. Saturn applies pressure. Pluto makes us emotionally uncomfortable. Uranus confronts us with wakeup calls. Surprises and upsets invite a re-evaluation of our course. Jupiter opens doors, offers us opportunities. Our job is to stay present, deeply listen, and follow what we hear from our heart.

Ideas on How to Approach Change

♥ Consider life-changing events and their challenges as part of your soul's journey. Prepare for something new with the goal of upgrading your quality of life.

♥ Identify where you have invested in being a victim and been entrenched in negativity and self-destruction. Get clear on what is your responsibility and what is not. Examine where and how your loyalty and obligations may be misplaced.

♥ You have free will and choice. How can you empower yourself? By taking action for yourself. Change something to change your attitude and energy — diet and exercise always help. Listen to your inner guidance to know where you need to make changes.

♥ Realignment from the superficial and unnecessary to more important and profound living is a long process. Work with yourself to allow old limitations to gradually fall away.

♥ Give yourself time. Proceed slowly but steadily. Be discerning and kind to yourself.

♥ It may sound trite, but it is true: learn your lessons, take advantage of opportunities when they present themselves, and be grateful to be alive at this time of the intense transition into the Aquarian Age.

Optimizing the Role of the Principal Players

The following discussion focuses on how we can optimize our relationship with the energies of the principal players in the 2020 lineups.

- ♦ **Jupiter and Sagittarius** expand the mind, our perspective, and our attitude.
- ♦ **Saturn and Capricorn** consolidate our energy and bring our ideas into manifestation.

Optimizing Jupiter ♃

Jupiter is about expansion, how we grow, understand life, and build faith in ourselves and our world. It is worthwhile to *identify the zodiac sign of our natal Jupiter.* The sign of our Jupiter indicates what we feel motivated to initiate and create and how we can best orchestrate our plans to be both successful and content with the results. The house placement of our Jupiter points to the arena of life where our Jupiter is most active.

Jupiter: Ruler of Sagittarius

The primary planet, or ruler, of Sagittarius is Jupiter. Jupiter was in its "home sign" of Sagittarius from December 2018 to December 2019, adding an optimistic feeling to our life. Many have been inspired to identify their life purpose and how they fit into the grand scheme of things.

Jupiter and Sagittarius are about discovering meaning and purpose in our life. If we are waiting for the weekend, planning only for a vacation, and basically trying to escape from our daily life, purpose and meaning are missing.

Jupiter in Capricorn

The nature of Jupiter's energy and lessons shifts when it moves into Capricorn on December 2, 2019. Jupiter in Capricorn helps us seriously assess what we are creating and how we are involved with the world. Its touchstones are personal impact and legacy. Jupiter in Capricorn is serious and keeps us on course for achieving self-mastery.

Jupiter's Nature and Gifts

Jupiter tends to be impulsive, naive, dogmatic, and even irrational. This is true especially when Jupiter is in the fire signs — Aries, Leo, and Sagittarius. In the earth signs — Taurus, Virgo, and Capricorn — Jupiter is more practical and thoughtful.

Jupiter brings opportunities, but it is up to us to grab them while the door is open. Our willingness to take action and our ability to see what is there are critical for taking advantage of Jupiter.

Jupiter energy encourages us to enhance things in our life and to enlarge our world in meaningful ways. With Jupiter in Capricorn, we are motivated to improve our physical, mental, and emotional health so that we have the strength and capacity to actualize our goals. We can feel more confident and self-assured when we wisely stabilize our financial situation.

Jupiter reminds us that the significance we accord to things shapes our thoughts, feelings, and life. How we interpret our life experiences dictates our mood and ability to attract. How we relate to our past creates the mold for our future. Are we a victim or a participant in a journey and a unique gift of life that unfolds? Do we grow in wisdom, compassion, and gratitude, or do we entrench ourselves in bitterness and regrets?

Jupiter Keeps Us on Purpose

Jupiter asks, What makes you feel alive, on purpose, and happy? What incites your passion and enthusiasm? What brings you joy and inspires you to keep going? Life is not always easy, but with Jupiter as our companion, we can feel fulfilled and grateful to be alive.

To optimize our Jupiter, we all need to look at how we limit ourselves by focusing on what is not possible, indulging in negativity, finding excuses, assuming the worst, and not valuing or prioritizing ourselves.

At a deep level, we each know what's right for us and are guided by our soul if we listen to our heart. Optimistic Jupiter reminds us not to let anyone talk, shame, or guilt trip us out of living our own life.

Our Internal Zeus

Jupiter is our internal Zeus who keeps all the other gods aligned toward our common goal.

In its awakened expressions, Jupiter is the cosmic lawyer devoted to uncovering the truth (not manipulating the facts to win). Finding the truth and using it to direct our actions are the winning strategy.

Jupiter can serve as our GPS, tracking where we are and where we are going. It can be our orienting and reorienting mechanism — optimally used to both determine our direction and to keep us pointed toward our destination. Jupiter is the unflinching arrow that keeps us on course.

We can use our Jupiter as our metal detector to help us find the gold. Pluto uncovers what is keeping us from finding the gold. We may have a Pluto breakdown before we can claim a Jupiter breakthrough.

Optimizing Saturn ♄

Saturn's domain is physical reality and the Earth. Saturn represents the laws of limitation and manifestation in the physical world. We have to pass Saturn's tests to awaken from our sleep state that is rooted in our unconscious personality and limited identity, which are attached to form. Saturn is a serious teacher as long as we live in unawakened ego-based consciousness.

Authority Through Discipline and Work

Saturn is about defining boundaries, establishing authority, and committing to what we value. Its energetic influence requires us to be realistic, responsible, and to play within the limits of time and space.

Saturn reminds us of the importance of self-discipline and efficient, productive use of our time and energy. As the taskmaster of the zodiac, Saturn teaches us that tenacity and a strong work ethic are important ingredients for success, promotion, and recognition in the world. Saturn is about what it takes to achieve status, hold a position of authority, be a respected leader, and live as a responsible human being.

Appreciating Saturn's Role

Astrologists and astrology enthusiasts sometimes complain about Saturn. Some people have a very negative view of Saturn and cringe when that aspect of their birth chart is discussed. With time and life experience, we gain an appreciation of the important role the Saturn archetype plays in our life. We do so by looking at what we have accomplished in our life and feel the sense of satisfaction and pride that goes with it. We can thank Saturn for the maturity that we have gained. We should take a moment to enjoy these feelings of accomplishment because we have worked for them.

The Saturn Principle

We must understand and learn to use the painful, yet ultimately empowering force of the Saturn principle, which provides the impetus to consolidate, establish boundaries, and create structural form. In its lower expressions, this restrictive force can be experienced as fear, pain, depression, feelings of lack, and oppressiveness, which prevent creation rather than making creation possible.

Instead of feeling imprisoned by life situations, we can use this energy to feel contained and centered in our own being.

If our psychological space is too narrow, we cannot awaken the light in our mind and heart. We can learn to relax so that we can release the emotional resistance that prevents us from experiencing our authentic nature. Instead of allowing our self-preservation instinct to shut down our life-giving impulses, we can use it to consolidate and protect our identity. We can liberate our creative instinctual powers that are bound up in subconscious programming and holding onto beliefs and situations that do not serve us by activating our Kundalini and raising our consciousness above the fear frequency.

Saturn and Maturity

Saturn appears difficult because it is about gaining maturity — about growing up in the physical world, which requires learning patience, being disciplined, taking responsibility, and being practical. As we get older and learn these basic lessons, Saturn becomes our friend and ally in manifesting our dreams, finding our place in the world, and earning a well-deserved lifestyle.

Redemption in the Aquarian Age

In the Piscean Age, under Saturn's rule, our ego had to be crucified, and we had to offer ourselves as martyrs to gain redemption. In the Aquarian Age, those who can transcend limited ego consciousness and awaken to their soul identity have a different path. By elevating and directing the personality to serve our soul self, we become a channel through which our soul can be expressed. We redeem ourselves by offering our unique contribution to serve love and participate in the awakening of planetary consciousness.

Saturn (the last planet visible to the naked eye) orbits at the boundary between physical and nonphysical reality. As an archetype, Saturn thus presents us with the challenge to pierce through the veil of illusion of separation. In the ring of Saturn, we find the light and bring that light into our own life.

Saturn and Jupiter

Saturn and Jupiter work together to define how we manifest and create in physical reality. Saturn obliges us to obey natural laws. Jupiter helps us get clear about our optimal direction and expansion when we align with cosmic laws. As a team, they guide our personal process of evolution and growth.

Optimizing Pluto ♇

The archetypal energies of Pluto help us penetrate deep into our psyche to align our personality with the integrity of our soul. Pluto requires honesty as it digs for the truth. Its terms are non-negotiable — we have to be real and realistic. Change is not easy in Pluto's unconscious and subconscious territory. But it is absolutely necessary for our personal growth and awakening to the reality of universal love.

Pluto's influence takes us into our lowest instincts where we are confronted by our unrecognized and controlling subconscious fears. Pluto looks under the outer circumstances to uncover the core issues that are blocking us from achieving our potential. In this way, it helps us uncover our essence and purpose for existence — to open our heart and to experience love.

Pluto exposes why we don't yet experience love and helps us break down the internal structures that get in the way. It is a slow evolutionary process to shift from loneliness to oneness, from dark to light, from unconscious to conscious. But these are our ultimate goals on planet Earth. Being in gratitude for the chance to make it to the light helps us get there.

Pluto and Saturn Together

Saturn and Pluto each in their own ways define what we have to deal with, let go of, and align with to reach our destination.

The archetypal energies of Saturn and Pluto speak to the most intense and difficult human challenges. Things can get very intense and difficult when they align. Saturn brings restriction and limitations to our present circumstances. Its serious work ethic encourages us to work hard. The message is to wisely direct our efforts and the use of our resources.[17]

We get directives from Pluto, who presses us to change attitudes and beliefs that have outlived their usefulness and become impediments to a better future and awakened consciousness. The transformation Pluto requires is a slow, deep, internal process. An upgraded inner foundation is necessary to build a renewed physical life (Saturn) rooted in spiritual connection.

Natal Saturn Conjunct Pluto

Saturn conjunct Pluto in our natal chart indicates hardship in our early years. This configuration is of course not present in everyone's chart. However, we may feel like it is a dominating force in 2020.

---

[17] Information in this section drawn from Jamie Partridge, "Saturn Conjunct Pluto – January 12, 2020," *Astrology King*, April 24, 2018. Retrieved from https://astrologyking.com/saturn-conjunct-pluto/

For those of us who have this configuration, our childhood was probably very challenging. Our parents may have been poor and struggling. Some kind of deprivation, restriction, or abuse influenced our beliefs and attitudes toward life and ourselves. We experienced some intense or prolonged hardship, abandonment, or loss that made us suffer but also caused us to become self-reliant and resourceful. Under harsh conditions, we learned to persevere and became determined to succeed in life. The gift is that we can face and endure hardship with a strong survival instinct that keeps us going.

Resist, Adapt, or Let Go

Saturn and Pluto can stubbornly resist change, which can perpetuate hard times. A major lesson to learn is that when faced with serious challenges and restrictive circumstances, we must know when to let go, change, and adapt to a new reality. We must also avoid self-depreciation, depression, and self-destructive habits that dig us further into suffer mode. Fear perpetuates fear.

Like my mother Ruth, with courage and grit, we can use these powerful energies to transform our life.

The 2020 Saturn Conjunct Pluto Transit

Moving through a Saturn conjunct Pluto transit requires hard work, patience, and tenacity. We may feel burdened by extra responsibilities — overly pressured, with not enough time, energy, and resources. Since the Saturn-Pluto conjunction has already been active within 2 degrees in 2019, we've become aware of some areas of our life that need more attention (health, family, relationships, finances, profession, etc.).

We are encouraged to get in touch with patterns, conditioning, behaviors, and beliefs that define how we view ourselves and the world. Something besides outer circumstances is holding us back and preventing us from moving forward. Saturn and Pluto invite us to identify what needs attention and to concentrate our efforts there.

Remember, Pluto grinds us on a slow, evolutionary process to create an internal foundation for a more conscious and meaningful life.

Embracing Your Personal Journey

Let Go of the Past

When major cycles end, we feel the need to complete or let go of relationships, activities, projects, and attitudes that have been the central focus of our life.

In some way, we each begin a new chapter in our life in 2020. The area of our birth chart being triggered by the three-planetary conjunction can help us see in what areas change will occur. Actually, we intuitively know. With three new planetary cycles being initiated in 2020, our first task is to let go of the past by finishing old projects, clean out what is no longer useful and relevant, and evaluate where we are now.

New Territory

When we start a new cycle, we enter new territory. We start over, enter a new period, or advance to another level. Before taking action, we need to consider where we want to go and how we can get there. We can set goals, but it is best to keep an open mind and a clear space for the new to be revealed.

The least beneficial approach is to try to run and hide. There is no place to hide, and if we try, we may miss some great opportunities. The optimal approach is to take a chance on ourselves, don't look back, and step forward into a new phase of our life.

Reoccurring Themes

Life is full of challenges. Certain themes reoccur or remain constant. There are patterns that define who we are, our life purpose, our path, and the nature of the experiences that we will have. Life presents us with what we need to learn and experience, not what we think we want.

We play out these themes so that over time we can find the gold of their higher expressions. A wise man calls this getting "the gifts from the garbage."

We become resilient, dynamic, and mature by using our creative potential and continuing to renew ourselves.

Letting Go of the Past in 2019 for 2020

The year 2019 initiated a tsunami of activity toward letting go and making room for something new in our life. Major themes for 2019 were cleaning out, tidying up, and preparing for the future. We cannot know exactly what the future will bring, but for sure we want to release as much excess baggage as possible to lighten our load.

During 2019, three cycles were in their final phase. We can experience endings in three different ways:

1. We can experience loss, sadness, or disappointment.
2. We can feel pressured to change against our will. There may be a strain on our finances or in our family.
3. We can resolve to take care of something, address an issue in our life, or adopt an attitude that we must change.

The bottom line is we won't be free until we allow the endings to happen or make the necessary changes.

We can also feel a sense of satisfaction that comes from completion, a job well done, an honest effort resulting in accomplishing our goals. We are content with our past and welcome what comes next. We feel prepared to enter a new unexplored phase of our life. We can feel an excitement about something new and different approaching. We may not know what the future brings, but we are positive about the possibilities.

How to Approach Change

There are many approaches to change. We can try to ignore the obvious and stubbornly refuse to change, but we will notice that resistance creates more difficulties. We can't get away with taking shortcuts or cheating. There is no way to hide by pretending, lying, or manipulation.

We learn as we go through a deep transformative process. While in the midst of a grueling makeover, it can be hard to be philosophical, willing to let go, and relax into the flow. However, we sabotage ourselves when we live in denial and avoid doing what we need to do.

We can also accept the inevitable and direct our attention and energy to doing what must be done. We can be guided by our desire for freedom, peace, and joy, which require honesty and willingness to be with what is.

Keep in mind, powerful forces are at play. Things are not going to stay the same. Don't resist taking responsibility for what you must do and who you are meant to be.

As best you can, accept change, relax, and go with the flow. Listen to your intuition and let your heart guide you. Become your own professional guide.

Whatever is broken, fix it or throw it out. Whatever you aren't using, give it to someone in need. As you let go of limiting factors, you clear the space for new doors to open. Use this transition time to prepare for your future.

Technology and the Heart

The technological revolution has dramatically altered how we live, but technology alone cannot rescue us from anger and fear and greed. We are being challenged to participate more fully in designing new structures that deal more effectively with all our global challenges.

We have to be able to operate from our heart for positive outcomes. We (men and women) have to work together with compassion for self and each other.

Chapter 7:
New Beginnings for the 12 Signs

Each zodiac sign sparks a different opportunity for new beginnings and new opportunities in 2020. The following are a few of the themes for each zodiac sign.[18] These possibilities can be relevant to our Sun sign, Moon sign, and planets in these signs and houses.

Aries and the First House

An identity makeover, which happens inside. An expanded sense of who you are and an awakening from limited ego to soul identity. A new lease on life and ability to love yourself.

Taurus and the Second House

A new approach to financial life, being more resourceful and managing material life more skillfully. Upgrading how you treat yourself and how you meet your needs. Examining what you really value and letting go of what you do not need.

Gemini and the Third House

Being more honest with self and others, improving communication skills, being cognizant of expectations and how they influence your choices and feed misperceptions. A new program to reduce stress and to strengthen your resilience and ability to process life events, including boundaries around how much you are sharing of your personal life.

Cancer and the Fourth House

Special attention to home and family. Renovation of home or change in living situation. Dedication to building a stable emotional inner reality from which to feel safe and confident in the world.

Leo and the Fifth House

A focus on how you want to use your energy. An amping up of creativity and self-expression. An awakening to and enjoyment in expressing your talents and gifts.

Virgo and the Sixth House

New regimes and making changes in daily routine to improve your health and fitness. Supporting your nervous system with deep breathing and meditation, and your body with good

---

[18] See Tem Tarriktar, "Looking Ahead, The Jupiter-Saturn-Pluto Conjunctions in 2020 for the 12 Signs," *The Mountain Astrologer*, December 2018–January 2019, p. 38ff.

nutrition and hydration. Not adding unnecessary stress from overworking and over-thinking. A more meaningful daily routine — being more present and appreciative of what you have.

Libra and the Seventh House

New and more meaningful close friendships and partnerships. New ways of presenting yourself and interacting that come from the recognition of what and how you are projecting onto others. (Others can feel uncomfortable in your presence, but they can't know what is going on in your head.) Awareness that what you project defines you in the eyes of others.

Scorpio and the Eighth House

New ways of dealing with finances and renewed business partnerships. Earning or receiving financial support from others to support long-term goals. Advancing personal partnerships to a deeper soulful level.

Sagittarius and the Ninth House

Launching a long-term endeavor related to higher and advanced education, spiritual growth, and/or travel. Changing the way you see the world and how you fit into the bigger picture. Letting go of beliefs and conditioning that brought you security in the past. Clearing your mind to feel more freedom.

Capricorn and the Tenth House

New career, personal authority, and position of power. The call of a new life mission. Clarifying your sense of mission by looking objectively at the big picture of your life in the collective.

Aquarius and the Eleventh House

New social activism and social responsibility that is nonconformist but serves a cause you believe in. Taking charge of whom you spend time with, evaluating friendships and groups you belong to.

Pisces and the Twelfth House

Increased compassion for the less fortunate. Devotion to your spiritual practice and connecting with a higher power. Trust. Let go and let God.

> *Pluto requires honesty* as it digs for the truth. Its terms are non-negotiable — we have to be real and realistic.

Chapter 8:
The Activating Angles in Your Horoscope

There are four activating angles in our horoscope.[19] These are the ascendant, descendant, nadir, and midheaven explained below and in the Appendix. These angles are activated when a planet transits the sign and degree of that angle, which is a function of the time it takes for a planet to move through the zodiac. For example, it takes Saturn 28-29 years to complete its journey through the zodiac. Therefore, Saturn will activate one of the four angles every 7 years. Because the outer planets (Uranus, Neptune, and Pluto) move slower, their activation of an angle is rarer and more significant. Activation by the inner planets (Mercury, Venus, and Mars) happens more often and thus the impact is shorter lived.

1. The Ascendant

The ascendant is the cusp of the first house, which is in the zodiac sign that was on the horizon when we are born. Our ascendant colors both how we look at the world and how we appear to others. It defines how we view reality and our approach to life, and it determines what drives our agenda.

When activated by planetary transits, the ascendant is the point of rebirth and serves to expand and awaken our sense of individual identity.

2. The Descendant

The descendant is opposite the ascendant and the cusp of the seventh house, which marks sunset. The zodiac sign on our descendant defines what we attract and seek in relationships.

In the domain of interpersonal relationships, we learn that each of our relationships is a looking glass, reflecting evolving parts of ourselves back to us so that we become more conscious, compassionate, and whole. What we don't like in someone else is a shadow part of ourselves until we can neutrally interact with empathy and compassion. What we seek in another, because we feel lacking in ourselves, must also be found inside by uncovering what has been suppressed or undeveloped.

Our descendant reminds us that love is ultimately an inside job, a state of being that we share with others. The more we integrate conflicting aspects of ourselves, the more love, peace, and beauty we have to share with everyone we are in relationship with.

When our descendant is activated by planetary transits, our personal relationships become a major focus and undergo transformation, which can include leaving unworkable relationships,

---

[19] See Frank C. Clifford, "Exploring the Midheaven in Your Horoscope. Part 1: Definitions," *The Mountain Astrologer*, December 2018–January 2019, 48–54.

upgrading existing ones, and forming brand-new relationships.

3. Nadir, or Imum Coeli (IC)

The sign on our nadir or Imum Coeli (IC) represents the type of energy that serves as an anchor and foundation for our inner world so that it can support us in the outer world. The zodiac energy of our IC represents our roots and instinctual self and what nurtures us.

We look at the sign of our midnight point to help us understand the underlying parental and psychological issues that drive us to succeed or to decline participation in the world.

We must be at peace with ourselves to thrive in the world. Our inner world is our greatest asset or saboteur. The extent to which we are not in alignment with the energy of our IC will manifest as our inability to effectively function in the world.

When our nadir is activated by a planetary transit, we are led to examine our inner world, our emotional state, and conditioning related to our parents and childhood.

IC and Cancer Archetype

In addition to the zodiac energy playing out in our fourth house (indicated by the sign on the IC), the general characteristics of the Cancer archetype operate. This is of special importance because the North Node (new territory to be developed) is currently in Cancer. The Cancer archetype helps us identify how our personal authority and values have been created by what was imprinted in our psyche as a child by our parents and family.

Planets in our fourth house and the sign of the IC indicate our emotional desires that direct our actions and goals in the world. The nature of our social involvement (or lack thereof) in the tenth house is rooted in what goes on behind the scenes in our invisible inner world that was formed in our childhood. It is the past that lives within us that has often been denied, shamed, and neglected.

Our Emotional Base

What we ignore and keep secret to ourselves is very often fear-based, which means that fear, sadness, and anger unconsciously steer our ship. Living in perpetual emotional crisis mode prevents us from achieving a sense of personal stability and security. It can also prevent us from achieving stability in other aspects of our life, including financial, social, and professional.

The emotional turmoil represented by our fourth house and the Cancer archetype can unconsciously prevent us from courageously interacting in the world. The North Node in Cancer urges us to pay attention to our inner reality and identify how it controls us. As we learn to acknowledge our inner needs, we become aware of how important it is to nurture ourselves so that our inner reality is able to support (not compromise) our outer reality. Self-love and emotional maturity then serve our social and professional roles and mission.

Optimally, while the North Node is in Cancer, we will hone our ability to trust our inner process, embrace what we feel, and develop inner confidence.

4. Midheaven

The sign of our midheaven (MC) defines how we appear "on stage" and are recognized in the world. Working with the sign on our midheaven is our best pathway to success professionally because it helps us identify the strategies, qualifications, and social skills we need in order to achieve recognition in the world.

Our MC helps us define our mission and instructs us on how to navigate our life. It guides us in figuring out where we are going and how to get there.

Our MC directs us to our destination and path to self-mastery, which is of course a lifelong process and linked to our success in the world. When we identify with and embody the qualities of the MC archetype, we attract opportunities and find peace with our role as our life unfolds.

We will discuss the midheaven in more detail below because it is also related to Capricorn and its ruler Saturn, which are the zodiac sign and planet related to the tenth house.

When our midheaven is activated, we more actively engage in our mission or professional life. We are challenged to define our goals and seriously work toward achieving them and the social recognition for doing so. At the midheaven, we leave our comfort zone, branch out on our own, and dare to take responsibility for our own life.

Success, Direction, and Destination

When we cross the midheaven into the tenth house, we have to examine our attitude toward success and how we achieve it. We explore the kind of success that gives us a sense of personal fulfillment.

When the most elevated point in our birth chart is activated by planetary transits, we often experience a change in life direction and reputation, get more clarity about our life path, and make life-changing career decisions.

Zodiac Sign on the Midheaven

It is important to identify the zodiac sign on our midheaven (MC). Our success in the world is achieved to the extent we embody the role or image symbolized by the MC. The archetype speaks for what we stand for, how we like to be known, and how we and others view our status and image. Below are a few keywords associated with how the zodiac signs on the MC present themselves to the world.

Aries — independence, self-determination
Taurus — strength found in persistence, determination, and sensuality
Gemini — ability to uplift through conscious communication
Cancer — kindness and nurturing
Leo — fun and passion for life

Virgo — the priest or priestess, independent authority
Libra — dedication to beauty, peace, and harmony
Scorpio — speaker and example of truth, moral integrity, and hard work
Sagittarius — leader sharing knowledge as a teacher, writer, speaker
Capricorn — conscience, sense of responsibility
Aquarius — nonconformist, free spirit
Pisces — compassion and love for all

Saturn Crossing the Midheaven

When Saturn crosses the midheaven, the high noon of the birth chart, we are driven to step out into the world, like it or not, ready or not. That we feel unready is a normal reflex to entering uncharted territory. Desiring to step up to the challenge is also a normal reflex. We have to test our inner strength and prove to ourselves and the world that we can be both effective and make an impact.

When Saturn crosses our MC, we are directed to examine to what extent we identify with the archetype on our MC and to become aware of how others see us as this archetypal role model.

Saturn crosses the midheaven at different times for everyone. How we deal with the challenges of being thrust into the world will vary according to our age. Young actors and athletes, for example, respond differently than older adults who have had more time to prepare and mature.

When our midheaven is activated, it is time to make changes that will have long-term effects on our life goals, reputation in public life, professional image, and success in the world.

Saturn's Impact on the Angles

It takes Saturn 29 and a half years to travel through the zodiac. Saturn transits to natal Saturn and Saturn's movement over the angles of our birth chart challenge us to question our current path and stir us to embrace a new relationship with ourselves, others, and our life. These are pivotal times to assess where we are going and why.

Saturn traveling through all the signs and the houses of the birth chart activates and demands that we deal with issues related to self-empowerment, personal responsibility, self-confidence, maturity, and independence. The most dramatic new beginning happens when Saturn crosses our ascendant and enters the first house.

A new phase begins and plays out in the next three houses. For example, the identity issues activated by Saturn transiting our ascendant will be played out in the first, second, and third houses. The intensity decreases as we deal with the issues at hand, adjust to new circumstances, and hone our inner reality to support a more viable outer reality.

The initial impact of transiting Saturn (and Pluto) as they reach the four angles of our birth chart can be dramatic. In 2020, Saturn is joined by Pluto, which increases the intensity of our new beginnings. Next, we identify if Saturn and Pluto are activating any angles of our birth chart.

Chapter 9:
How to Read Your Birth Chart and Transits

If you want to dive deeper and actually learn how to read your horoscope and identify how the transiting planets are impacting you, the next part of this book is for you. Studying your birth chart and transits often serves to confirm what you already know intuitively.

There are a lot of pieces, but once you familiarize yourself with the basics, you can start fitting all the pieces together. We are each a fascinating combination of energies and archetypes that express during our lifetime. I am still learning and enjoying the *ah-ha!* moments that come with each additional revelation.

Start out with one piece and stick with it until you are ready to add another piece. I have listed the steps below. The following focuses on the 2020 transits and how they impact us.

How to Read Your Chart and Transits

Your Birth Chart

1. Create and print your birth chart from an online source and use it to complete the following steps.[20]
2. Identify the **zodiac sign** of your Sun, Moon, and each planet in your birth chart.
3. Identify the **house placement** of your Sun, Moon, and each planet.
4. Identify the **degree** of the zodiac sign of your Sun, Moon, and each planet.
5. Determine whether your Sun, Moon, and any planet is placed on or within 2-3 degrees of the **four angles of the chart:** (1) ascendant — cusp of first house, (2) nadir — cusp of fourth house, (3) descendant — cusp of seventh house, (4) midheaven — cusp of tenth house.

Current Locations of Planets — Transits

1. Study the chart of the January 12 Saturn-Pluto Conjunction (see next page).
2. Notice that Saturn and Pluto are at 23 degrees Capricorn.
3. The South Node is also in Capricorn opposite the North Node (not noted in the chart).

---

[20] You can find a website that generates free birth charts by doing a search for "natal birth chart" in Google.

4. Notice that the North Node is in Cancer opposite the South Node.

Identify Where the Capricorn Planets Fall in Your Birth Chart

1. Find the house where Capricorn resides in your birth chart.
2. Identify if your Sun, Moon, and any natal planets that are within 2-3 degrees of 23 degrees Capricorn.
3. Also identify any other planets that are at or near 22-24 degrees of another sign.
4. Notice if any angles of your birth chart fall at 20-26 degrees Capricorn.
5. The angles and house that contain Capricorn are where new beginnings will be activated in your life.
6. The planets that are within 20-26 degrees Capricorn will be the most affected and supercharged for a new beginning.

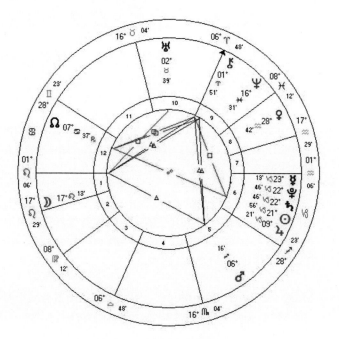

Saturn-Pluto Conjunction 2020
Jan. 12, 2020, 16:49 GMT
London, UK

Identify Where Cancer Plays Out in Your Birth Chart

1. Find the house where Cancer resides in your birth chart. This will be opposite Capricorn.
2. Identify your Sun, Moon, and any natal planets that are within 2-3 degrees of 23 degrees Cancer.
3. The house that contains Cancer will be challenged to transform.
4. The Sun, Moon, and planets that are within 20-26 degrees Cancer will be the most affected.
5. The house and planets in Cancer need you to work on Capricorn lessons to create healing and move into their power.

Pluto-Jupiter Conjunctions at 22 and 24 Degrees Capricorn

Since the Pluto-Jupiter conjunctions happen at 22 and 24 degrees Capricorn, the same investigation as above applies. This time around you will be more proficient and able to incorporate an understanding of how Jupiter's enthusiasm and expansiveness affect you differently than Saturn's heaviness.

Orbs of Influence
I have chosen to use 3 degrees as the orb of influence. As explained in the introduction, the approaching planet will begin to influence the natal planet several degrees before it actually aligns with the exact degree. Its influence will wane as it distances itself.

Who Is Impacted When?

For those who have Capricorn on the four angles, or who have Saturn, Pluto, and other planets at 22-24 degrees Capricorn, the 23-degree Saturn-Pluto Capricorn conjunction and the Pluto-Jupiter conjunctions will be the most impactful. Although, wherever 22-24 degrees Capricorn falls in your birth chart will be impacted.

Those with planets near 22-24 degrees Cancer will be awakened through opposition, which means that your inner-emotional reality (Cancer) needs attention to support your activities in the world.

Planets near 22-24 degrees Aries and Libra will be confronted with choices through squares or 90-degree angles. Squares require evaluation, choice, decisions, and action.

Announcing Your New Beginning

The Jupiter, Saturn, and Pluto alignments occur in the last 8 degrees of Capricorn and the 1st degree of Aquarius. Planets in our birth chart in these degrees will be the most sensitive to the energies.

Summary of Degrees of the Three Conjunctions

1. January 12, 2020: Pluto meets Saturn at 23 degrees Capricorn.
   Pluto and Saturn have been within 2 degrees (21-22) for most of 2019.

2. Spring 2020: Pluto meets Jupiter in Capricorn at 22 degrees Capricorn and then at 24 degrees.
   March 29–April 5: both in 24 degrees Capricorn
   June 22–June 30: both in 24 degrees Capricorn (Jupiter is retrograde)
   November 7–November 13: both in 22 degrees Capricorn

3. December 21, 2020: Saturn and Jupiter meet at 1 degree Aquarius.

Pluto Transits

Pluto transits are the deepest and most penetrating psychological transits.

Pluto is transiting 21-23 degrees Capricorn from mid-January 2019 through mid-February 2020. The Pluto pressure remains in 24 degrees Capricorn (with retrograde back into 23-22 degrees) through January 2021.

To assess the astrological meaning, symbolic implications, and practical impact for your own life, identify where these degrees of Capricorn and Aquarius fall in your birth chart.

Below are specific dates and ages that will be impacted.

Sun-Saturn Cycles

Sun-Saturn is the most significant structural cycle because it deals with taking responsibility for ourselves and our life. We seek meaning and purpose and focus on building both inner and outer structures in our life to express our authentic selves.

This time, the new Sun-Saturn cycle presents those with Sun (or ascendant) at or near 23 degrees Capricorn with a double whammy because Pluto is also involved in the new cycle.

Were You Born January 9–15? A New Sun-Saturn-Pluto Cycle

Those with Sun in Capricorn will be initiated into a new Sun-Saturn-Pluto cycle during Saturn and Pluto's passage through Capricorn from 2018 through January 2020.

If you were born on January 12, the Pluto-Saturn conjunction will be directly on your Sun. If you were born within 3 degrees (January 9–15), the Capricorn alignments will occur close to your natal Sun. Being on or close (within 3 degrees) activates new and significant personal cycles between your Sun and transiting Saturn and Pluto.

A Shift in Life Direction
Your basic life direction and foundations of personal truth and integrity will be dramatically altered in a deep purging and death-rebirth process.

Jupiter in Capricorn will pass over your natal Sun three times in 2020. This can increase optimism, add psychological strength, and present one with new social opportunities. A forced and perhaps dramatic ending of your previous lifestyle and path will lead to a serious assessment of where you are headed, how you can overcome obstacles, and a desire to open yourself to new possibilities.

Were You Born January 20–23?

If you were born between January 20 and 23 (in the first degrees of Aquarius), the timing and sequence of your three new Sun cycles happen in a different order.

The Jupiter-Sun and Saturn-Sun conjunctions happen first, simultaneously in December 2020. You will be dealing with both the demands and opportunities related to real-life issues.

The death-rebirth/purging of the Pluto-Sun conjunction will occur three years later, in 2024 when Pluto has entered Aquarius.[21]

Saturn Return for Those Born 1932, 1961, and 1990

Those with natal Saturn in late Capricorn and early Aquarius (born 1932, 1961, and 1990) will be experiencing their third, second, and first Saturn returns respectively, which are major transitions in life. Adding Jupiter and Pluto to the mix intensifies the impact and opens them up to life-changing experiences that activate hidden potentials.

Natal positions of other planets that are in close alignment to the degree where one of the cycles begins will also be significantly affected. Simultaneous multi-planet transits can be dramatically impacted. For example, if your Sun, Mercury, and Venus are within a few degrees of each other, they will all be affected and thus your experience will be intensified.

You will need to identify the degree and zodiac position of the planets in your natal chart to see this clearly.

Are You in Your Mid to Late 60s?

Those born in the early to mid-1950s, who are now in their mid to late 60s, all share the natal configuration of Saturn and Neptune conjunct Libra square Uranus in Cancer near the 23-degree cardinal trigger point of the Saturn-Pluto conjunction in Capricorn.[22]

This natal configuration implies that these people are sensitive to the dreams and aspirations of their cultures, either for the "good life" or material well-being and intimate relatedness, or for the transcendent ideals of spirituality. They wish to participate harmoniously, often "going along to get along." And yet that intention is disrupted, time and again, either by their own willful demand for independence and separateness, or by other people's judgments about their lack of acceptability. The security of belonging is at war with the need for independence or uniqueness within their psyches. Fitting in versus standing apart is a lifelong conflict for them.

Mid-to-late-60s folk will experience a cascading set of six personal outer planet transits as a major T-square is formed. The timing and sequence of the transits will vary according to the placement of the natal planets. Loss of security (whether feared or literal) or disillusionment with former ideals is a distinct possibility.[23]

These people need to cultivate a strong base of inner security and self-confidence in their unique contribution. This is the time that they can choose to take action and offer their gifts to the world.

Were You Born in 1974–76, 1982–84, 1998–99?

Those born in 1974–76, 1982–84, and 1998–99 will experience four personal outer planet transits, two from Saturn and two from Jupiter. You will feel the need to resolve an underlying

---

[21] Herbst, 35.
[22] Ibid., 36.
[23] Ibid.

tension between material and spiritual desires and goals. Changes in circumstances will require and help you adapt so that you can unleash your creativity and discover new ways to participate in planetary transformation.

- Born 1974–76 (age: 40s) — Saturn and Uranus
- Born 1982–84 (age: mid-30s) — Saturn and Pluto
- Born 1998–99 (age: 20s) — Saturn and Neptune[24]

1 Degree Aquarius

More insights will be forthcoming later in 2020 as the Saturn-Jupiter conjunction at 1 degree Aquarius approaches. Jupiter will challenge Saturn's conservative tenacity to hold on to the practicality of supporting the status quo.

Aquarius invites us to be okay with feeling different, and even excluded, to offer our unique contribution. Aquarius challenges us to get unstuck from the past. We can't hold on to the same paradigm and transform. Breakthroughs come at the price of trying something new.

Personal transformation always takes us into unfamiliar territory. Crazy ideas fuel breakthroughs that lead us to the next frontier. We have to continue to look at the root causes, not the symptoms, to understand the dynamics of creating a new future. We will have to get used to the inevitable tension between holding on and letting go. And then courageously engage in what is next.

> ***We are each a fascinating combination of energies and archetypes*** that express during our lifetime. Happiness is enjoying our life-long journey of self-knowing and exploration.

---

[24] Above discussion drawn from Herbst, 35-36.

Chapter 10:
Living and Awakening with Saturn and Pluto

Human life is by its very nature challenging and always changing. When Saturn and Pluto join together and their transits interact with our birth chart (our energy, emotions, beliefs, and daily life), we need to be forewarned that radical shifts may be forthcoming.

Summarizing Some Basics

Saturn's View of Life Is Pragmatic
Saturn takes about 29½ years to cycle through the zodiac. Saturn's view is pragmatic and in touch with the dynamics of living on planet Earth. Saturn represents the outer circumstances in our life that force us to (1) look deeply at why they are happening, (2) understand the phases of change, and (3) grow into a mature adult.

Pluto Views Life from Afar
It takes Pluto about 248 years to cycle around the Sun and through the zodiac. Pluto views reality from the outer reaches of the solar system. Pluto's vast scope and distant position beyond what makes sense to us. It takes deep observation to penetrate Pluto's existential truths.

Archetypes Are Our Teachers
As the celestial bodies (Sun, Moon, other planets, and asteroids) move through the zodiac signs, they express the energies and the lessons represented by the zodiac archetypes. By studying the archetypes of both the planets and the 12 signs, we get in touch with the nature of the messages, moods, tests, and lessons that prevail as they play out and are activated by transits to planets in our birth chart. We gain a greater understanding of ourselves, others, and life.

Cycles, Our Birth Chart
Our birth chart defines the parameters within which we develop, create, evolve, and become whole. Certain cycles recur throughout our life. For example, we all go through our first Saturn return between age 28 and 30 and our second Saturn return between 58 and 60. However, the specific circumstances, issues, and reactions of each individual are unique.

Our Soul's Journey Is an Evolutionary Process
There is always old fear-based ego conditioning to be released and new unexamined parts of ourselves to be examined. In response, we typically experience both resistance to change and the disquieting awareness that the old status quo is being challenged and undergoing change whether we like it or not.

Challenges and dissatisfaction lead to evaluation. Evaluation leads to motivation to change. Motivation leads to action. Action creates transformation. We are enriched and become more conscious. We get closer to experiencing our true soul essence.

Saturn and Pluto

A Daunting Pair: Saturn and Pluto

Saturn Works with Visible, Physical Reality
Saturn works on the physical level in identifiable real-world circumstances. Through our life challenges, Saturn externalizes what is going on in our subconscious. We are confronted with actual experiences so we can see *what* we are manifesting.

Pluto Works with Invisible Influences
Pluto works internally so that we get in touch with *how* we are manifesting. Pluto offers the possibility of clearing and elevating our internal reality so that we can change what we manifest.

Saturn and Pluto Work Together to Make Our Unconscious Conscious
Together Saturn and Pluto oblige us to experience what is happening and figure out a strategy to deal with both our inner reality and our outer situation as follows:

1. Pluto works on the unconscious level and subtle dimensions of reality.
2. Pluto exposes how our inner reality creates our outer reality.
3. Saturn makes sure that we see and feel what we are projecting.
4. Pluto makes sure that we examine the beliefs, attitudes, and conditioning that determine what we project and thus create in the world. Pluto allows no hypocrisy.

The Awakening and Maturation of Self
Saturn helps us build a consolidated sense of self (a mature ego) that is capable of managing our life situations.

Pluto challenges our childish immature ego. We may feel that our identity is being threatened and that our very existence is at stake. This is a natural reaction to the awakening process as we evolve from limited ego to soul consciousness.

> **Who is the savior?** It is your own higher consciousness which can save you from your own lower consciousness.
> – Yogi Bhajan

A Realistic Approach to Life

Debilitating Attitudes About Perfection

For many unfortunate reasons, humans have bought into a debilitating belief system (i.e., lie) that we are supposed to be perfect, that we should be able to figure everything out and never make mistakes. With these attitudes, our self-esteem is always getting a beating. In so many ways, we have been programmed to feel insecure, to doubt ourselves, and believe that we are not good enough.

The truth is that our soul incarnates on planet Earth to learn through exploration and experience. It is obvious that we can't already know everything. We have to figure things out as we go. Everyone's life is complicated. We only see what we can see in the moment based on our past and our level of awareness.

Saturn teaches us that we never reach perfection in human life. We keep going and continue to evolve. There is always more. Our human life is designed to present us with situations and challenges for us to learn, grow, mature, and excel so we can become the authority in our own life. We gain a deep sense of well-earned satisfaction as we go through our tests and meet our life challenges.

From Fear-Based Duality to Love

The chaos of duality and the impediments imposed by the dense fear-based environment in which we live has made it almost impossible to be ourselves and to work in harmony with others. Moving into the heart chakra energies and higher frequencies of love is providing us with the space to be much more functional, cooperative, and harmonious.

The dynamic interaction between Pluto and Saturn is currently awakening us to how we can move into the vibration of love and oneness. When our individual being (body, mind, emotions, senses, and free will) aligns with the cosmic energies, it becomes possible to align in oneness in physical reality with the universal force that is embodied in each of us. It becomes possible to live and learn from love.

Our Personal Life Journey

Our personal journey is about our evolutionary development through life. As we weave our way through the labyrinth of life, we create our own tapestry, which we can only fully appreciate at the end of our journey — when our soul exits our body and leaves this incarnation.

Our human journey is filled with hopes, dreams, fantasies, aspirations, tests, surprises, trepidation, disappointments, satisfaction, joy, and myriad variations on these themes.

Above all, our human life is full of challenges and lessons on how to deal with them. We each have to find our own formula. We move through many phases of life and planetary cycles. Our individual situation depends on many factors, including age, circumstances, attitude, and previous conditioning and experiences.

A New Perspective: Seeing G-O-D

The modern world has tended to place us between a hot place of illusionary fantasy and harsh practical reality. This existential dilemma is the result of the perceived separation between our human existence and the divine oneness of all existence.

Beliefs are no longer sufficient to work our way through this dilemma; they ensnarl us in mental fixations that keep us engulfed in negative spaces that prevent our elevation into consciousness. An expanded personal experience is needed, where we no longer have to rely on supplication to an external god or wander aimlessly in nihilism.

What we need is another perspective — one that makes every aspect of life meaningful and sacred. A primary goal of the Aquarian Age is to acquire an expanded experience of life where our personal journey is seen in the context of our oneness with all life and dimensions of reality.

Conscious participation in the cycles of life is what opens our perceptive gates to G-O-D, the G — generating, O — organizing, and D — delivery system of creation. (See Introduction.)

That which is at first hidden is revealed. That which is pragmatic becomes sacred.

The Saturn-Pluto Role in Transformation

Understanding and experiencing the interactive relationship between our internal and external realities are prerequisites for bringing the unconscious into consciousness and achieving our personal alchemy.

Saturn and Pluto are key players in this transformational process. Saturn deals with basic needs. Pluto digs deeper into existential needs. By participating consciously in the basic activities of daily life, we uncover, understand, and satisfy both our external and internal needs.

So much of what is interpreted negatively about our ego can be refined during our human journey to deliver us to an integration of all parts of ourselves and to elevate our expressions to love-based instead of fear-based drivers.

Our immature ego (unawakened self) evolves as we develop an identity structure that is a practical director and a soul-inspired instrument of our soul.

Basic Themes of Saturn's Approach to Life

1. Bound by Laws
Saturn lives on the border between physical and nonphysical reality, between the finite and the infinite, bound by immutable laws that prevail in both kingdoms. We are subject to the

unchanging laws in a reality that is always changing and ever in motion. At the threshold of potential and infinite possibilities, we are subject to limits and circumscribed by the boundaries of physical reality.

2. Transformation, Not Transcendence
Saturn is not about transcendence into the nonphysical dimension of reality. Saturn is about transformation so that we can see the transcendent in the physical world. Saturn is ultimately about seeing divine perfection in an inherently imperfect world.

3. Time and Cycles
Saturn is about time and space, but not the oppressive limits of time. Saturn is about tuning in to and accepting divine timing. It is about awakening to the cycles of life, recognizing when something is over, when a change of direction is needed, and when a new beginning beckons. Saturn is about appropriate, timely, and inevitable change.

4. Self-Definition
Saturn is about self-definition. We define ourselves through experience. Through experience, we gain insight and wisdom. The maturing process prepares us for the future. We perpetually live in the now, between the past and the future.

5. Past, Limits, Attachments
Saturn themes center on facing the past, the old, limits, and attachments so that what is not useful can be released and what is yet undeveloped can be explored and nurtured into being.

Saturn Transits: Realistic Management of Our Life

Each planet is part of our orientation mechanism. Saturn helps orient our journey in relationship to the events in our life.[25] How we deal with situations is a determining factor for self-evaluation of our worth, position, and power in the world. Saturn is about making our life manageable given the limitations, constraints, and cosmic and natural laws that we must adhere to in physical reality. Ultimately, Saturn is a very good friend.

Below, I discuss some of the ways that Saturn gets our attention and orients us toward healing from the inside out.

Contradictory Dynamics

Saturn confronts us with contradictory dynamics. Worrisome events create external challenges; for example, loss of employment, financial duress, and illness. Our Saturn tests make us aware of the boundaries between the unconscious and the conscious. We can be initially shocked at the loss of a job, but the truth is that we didn't like the situation and wanted out. If we wait too long to devise our own exist strategy, the Universe devises one for us.

---

[25] Erin Sullivan, *Saturn in Transit: Boundaries of Mind, Body, and Soul* (Boston: Weiser Books, 2020). This brilliant book offers rich insights into the workings of Saturn.

Externalization of Complex Patterns

Externalization of complex patterns is how we become aware of what has been normalized (and hidden) in our unconscious. Sometimes it takes a shocking situation to make us aware of what we have systematically suppressed. Saturn and Uranus help us out.

Changing Our Inner Reality

Our inner reality must change in order to adapt and find resolution to our life challenges. Our tendency to preserve and conserve is not workable under the pressure of changed circumstances. We must expand our mind to consider uncomfortable options and be willing to move into unknown territory; that is, we must go within to access and deal with our outer situation. Gradually we learn to address our circumstances with neutrality and not fall into self-criticism or be overtaken by victim interpretations of events.

A Time of Testing and Inner Grit

Saturn transits are a time for testing and building our inner grit. They are not a time to wallow in self-pity, escapism, or denial. From introspection, we must rise to the occasion and deal consciously and as effectively as possible with what life has dealt us. The inner call is to further self-development, growth, and maturity.

Saturn as an Interface Between the Personal and Impersonal Planets

Because Saturn orbits between the inner and outer planets, it is the interface planet between our personal and transpersonal realities. Saturn brings into our awareness the larger meaning of life events as they evolve in the context of cycles. From the perspective of Saturn's 29-year cycle, we gain meaning and are better able to accept, adjust to, and navigate our current phase of life. We need to see the totality to not be discouraged, avoid discounting important details as meaningless, and not fall into interpreting our life events as either bad karma or luck.

External and Family Demands

The placement of Saturn in the birth chart can play out as pressure to take care of others' needs at the expense of our own. Saturn makes us look at how as an adult we have inherited unresolved family issues. External demands of parents and other authority figures can cause us to diminish our own importance, suppress our individuality, and inappropriately sacrifice ourselves, our personal needs, and happiness. This is especially true for women.

Saturn transits bring this past conditioning up to be healed so we can be liberated to follow our own path without guilt, shame, or external opinions about what we "should" be or do. As we become aware of how we have compromised ourselves and compensated to fit into dysfunctional patterns, we can absolve ourselves of further unreasonable responsibility, free ourselves, and stop passing on these patterns to our children.

Saturn and the Outer Planets

When Saturn transits the natal placement of one of the outer planets (Uranus, Neptune, and

Pluto), circumstances that present themselves have deep meaning, which we must pay attention to and unravel. We are well advised to not take whatever is happening lightly because how we react, how we interpret, and how and why we make choices at this juncture will affect us the rest of our life. These are decisive moments that create our future. We are simultaneously aware of the dynamics of time — past, present, and future.

Integrating Themes: Control/Awareness and Gain/Loss

Saturn challenges our need to control. We cannot be in control of outcomes. But we can be present to what is happening within and without and make adjustments, which bring inner transformation and connection with the will of our soul.

The dynamic between limitation and expansion, which are both present, force us to be realistic. Loss and gain are also always themes of growth and transformation. What we gain is so much more important than what we initially feel we are losing.

Resistance and Letting Go

Resistance is also always a part of Saturn and our psyche. However, the deeper we connect with our inner reality and find a stable foundation within, the easier it is to let go of resistance and allow inevitable change to occur.

No Sugarcoating Saturn's Effects

There is no way to sugarcoat Saturn. Our attention is drawn to something that is unresolved and must be dealt with. Discomfort and feeling oppressed are natural reactions. Loss of energy, which is intensified when we resist, is a typical effect of Saturn. Our vitality will return in a more consolidated form after Saturn moves on and we have acquired a more stable sense of self.

A Weight Is Lifted

Saturn is heavy. The best thing about Saturn transits is when they are over. We feel a sense of relief. A weight has been lifted. A burden has disappeared. We feel lighter and less encumbered. We have actually pushed a rock up to a new plateau. We have gained something, and we have earned it! We have acquired inner strength, fortitude, and stamina that we can take with us. It's time to enjoy the respite before the next rock confronts us on our path.

> *Saturn is about making our life manageable within realistic constraints.*

Pluto Transits

Existential Dilemmas as Wakeup Calls

For many, Pluto transits are like a kiss of death. Pluto presents us with existential dilemmas: How can we work with what is out of our control? How do we deal with mortality and death, actual and cyclical?[26] Ultimately, Pluto is about waking us up, but this does not happen without a certain degree of suffering, crisis, and pain. We are not magically transformed without some deep existential anguish. There is no way to euphemistically gloss over how we will experience a Pluto transit.

In sum, transformation for Pluto is not a superficial affair. For Pluto, the goal of transformation is to connect deeply to the space of love within. We can deal with Pluto transits from the perspective of an "opportunity" to engage deeply in the spiritual alchemy of our soul and how we wake up from unconscious to conscious existence.

Keep in mind that transits pass and do not last forever. There is always a promise of a new life when they are over (if we do our inner work).

Saturn, Pluto, and the Transcendent

Saturn is not about transcendence into the nonphysical dimension of reality. Saturn is about transformation so that we can see the transcendent in the physical world.

Pluto is about clearing out the subconscious programming so that we can actually be consciously present to the dynamic dance of the infinite in the finite.

---

[26] Dena DeCastro, "Pluto Transits: Alchemy and Initiation," *The Mountain Astrologer*, June–July 2019, 60–65.

Chapter 11:
Saturn and Pluto Through the Houses and Signs

The following discussion can be relevant to our Sun sign, Moon sign, and planets in these signs and houses.

While we are on planet Earth, there is always pressure, questions, more to explore, more to become, more ways to participate, and more to digest, integrate, and enjoy. We are better off if we get used to and accept this nature of Earth School and embrace all aspects of life while we are here. We won't be here forever. There will never be another you or a life like yours.

Life is about learning to deal with what happens in the moment and sticking with what needs to be addressed until answers come and we are able to appropriately respond. We earn treasures as our emotional and physical bodies relax and our mind is awakened.

Key Karmic Challenges

The sign and house placement of Saturn and Pluto in our horoscope indicate our key karmic challenges this lifetime, which prod us to wake up and stay awake. Actually, our whole horoscope delineates our formula for working out our karma so we can awaken. (I like the idea that karma simply indicates we have more to learn.) The day of our birth sets our journey into motion.

Gradually we become aware of our unfulfilled desire for love. Our spiritual path is about breaking down the wall between our physical desire for love and our primal need to experience higher universal love. The anguish of separation and emptiness fuel our desire to experience what is not yet accessible. We realize that something is preventing us from having what we desire the most. As our suffering increases, our motivation to awaken intensifies. We turn to meditation and quiet moments to connect with the space where love resides.

Saturn Through the Houses and Zodiac

Saturn transiting through the signs and houses presents challenges designed to help us crystallize our rough diamond into radiant light.

Saturn spends two and a half years in each zodiac sign, during which time it passes through one or two houses.

Houses and Signs 1–6
The 14-plus years of the 29-year Saturn cycle that transpire under the horizon line is where we

move from an unconscious state into more conscious awareness of who we are and of the gifts we have retrieved.

The first six houses and zodiac signs are about the development of personal identity, worth, strength, and skills. The first three houses deal with unconscious development and initiate building skills for making our unconscious conscious.

The first six houses incorporate the developmental aspects of our human journey that prepare us to interact in the world in phases 7–12.

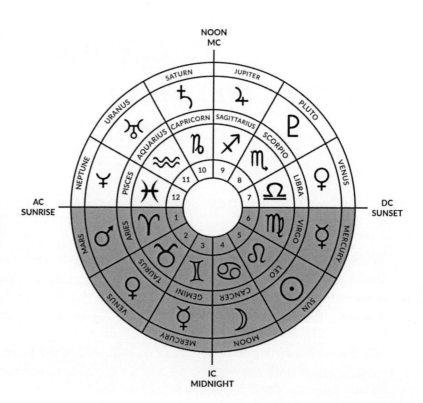

Houses and Signs 7–12
The 14-plus years of the 29-year Saturn cycle that transpire above the horizon line happen in the daylight of everyday life.

In houses 7–12, we are tested and grow in our relationship to the external world.

The 12 Houses

Each of the 12 houses represents an arena and phase of our human journey. The respective zodiac sign they are associated with engages specific challenges and helps us seek answers, find resolution, and become more empowered. These basic themes play out in everyone's life. The following discussion explains the Saturn and Pluto dynamics in each house and sign.

In many people's birth chart, Saturn and Pluto are in different houses. That doesn't mean that they don't interact. They just interact in a different way than in the intense collaboration of the 2020 conjunction. Here we discuss how they are currently working together to catapult us into waking up.

Challenges and Lessons to Learn

Life presents us with challenges related to each house and zodiac sign. Our birth chart indicates specific areas and themes that will play out and how we can learn from these encounters with life.

Ongoing Unfoldment
Life as represented by the 12 houses and zodiac signs is a progressive and ongoing unfoldment that lasts our lifetime. It is a slow evolutionary process to bring the unconscious into

consciousness. Retrieval of what was repressed, forgotten, or simply dormant until the right time for its discovery is the norm for human development.

Self-empowerment requires self-examination. Continued denial and repression swallow us in the past, preventing us from tapping into our inner treasures and unlocking deeper levels of our potential and creativity.

Feeling Stuck in Saturn
With Saturn in any house, we often feel stuck. We sometimes experience that progress is being delayed or impeded by an unidentifiable force. But actually we are being prodded to dig deep and stay present to our feelings and emotions that arise so we can build a conscious inner foundation that supports us in moving forward. We explore and initiate ourselves as we come home to ourselves and find our roots.

The Hunger and the Nourishment
Saturn energy feels heavy. We may feel a loss of energy wherever Saturn is placed in our birth chart or transiting. Limited physical energy is accompanied by an emotional and spiritual hunger for something we can't identify. Self-nurturing helps us find what we are looking for — a source of sustenance within. As we feel nourished by it, defense systems formed early in life can be replaced by self-love and acceptance. Feelings of vulnerability no longer need to be interpreted as weakness and can instead lead us to open our heart to ourselves.

Feeling Insecure with Pluto
Insecurity is a normal human emotion, especially when we begin a new phase of our life. Awareness of our insecurities leads us to explore what has been imprinted in our psyche that is not a secure foundation. Pluto's influence can add to our existential malaise. We can feel disconnected, disoriented, and not sure of what we should do next.

As we are able to expose and discard the undercurrents of hidden agendas, we become more authentically ourselves. We move from unconscious behavior and identity to self-awareness and conscious choice and free will.

The Sequence
Each successive house and sign add to our tool chest. Each offers us strategies to further the development, maturity, and experience of our soul in physical reality. When we experience a limitation, we can look to the next zodiac sign and house for ways to expand and explore human life.

Learning with Saturn and Pluto in Capricorn

Each of the 12 houses focuses on what we have to learn to access our power and grow into a consciousness of inner peace and contentment. Saturn and Pluto are not warm fuzzy teachers. In Capricorn, they become even more serious. So don't expect an easy ride. The good news is that the serious work required is rewarded with deep satisfaction at the end of the journey. If we maintain an attitude of gratitude for the opportunity to travel the distance to experience inner peace and love, we can also appreciate and even enjoy each step of the way.

First House/Aries: Identity and Personal Existence

Ascendant Is a New Beginning

When any of the outer planets (Pluto, Neptune, Uranus) and Saturn cross our ascendant, we are launched into a new beginning, a rebirth of our identity, and the start of a new cycle that deepens our experience of life. (See the discussion of the ascendant in chapter 8.)

The First House and Aries

From Mystery to Self-Knowing

In the first house, we gradually gather pieces of our identity and fit them together to create a coherent sense of self and self-image. Awakening to our soul identity is a slow process because we are born a mystery to ourselves. We must retrieve our essence from our unconscious and make it consciously known and expressed. Our relationship with ourselves will emerge from the obscurity of the yet unformed soul self as we let go of false personas and become more authentically who we are. We gradually build a self-image and projection that aligns with and expresses our soul.

Issues and Gifts

Issues and lessons in the first house concern self-centeredness, self-confidence, impulsiveness, impatience, anger, and assertiveness. We are challenged to survive by reaching deeper levels of self-definition. It is normal to feel self-protective as we try to figure out whom we are protecting and why.

Some of the many gifts that we awaken and develop relate to self-discipline, courage, and fearlessness. As we become more self-aware, we learn how our presence and projection impact what we create and attract.

Saturn and Pluto Challenges in the First House

Rehabilitation, regeneration, and rebirth are apt terms to describe what we experience when Saturn and Pluto transit our ascendant and our first house and activate issues that require us to explore our personal identity. Saturn and Pluto in the first house require introspection, which obviously brings up old wounds and misunderstandings. Through self-examination, we gain insight into our limited ego-driven habitual behavior patterns and survival strategies.

Expanding Our Identity Structure

Superficial, immature, ego-oriented definitions and positions titter on unstable ground. Our quest for self-definition is a long process to create a stable foundation from which to operate and evolve in the world.

Challenges to Our Identity

Any challenge to who we think we are is naturally threatening. But put in perspective, we can gradually let go of false masks and discover more authentic replacements. The "death" process is accompanied by a rebirth or an expansion into self-knowledge and self-authority.

As we uncover the moods and attitudes that affect the energy we project, we recognize hidden emotional undercurrents that control us. As we cease to construct our identity from false masks, our energy can flow, our essence can surface, and we become more authentic, magnetic, and real.

Self-Initiation and Self-Discovery
Our process of self-initiation includes discarding what does not align with our soul blueprint. We redefine and renegotiate who we are by going deeper into our soul qualities, leaving superficial and externally imposed concepts behind. We discover our authentic identity as we progressively replace externally imposed imprints with our master blueprint.

By investigating our soul blueprint as set out in our birth chart, which depicts how our soul interacts with the world and the cosmos, we discover optimal ways to operate in this incarnation. Our soul searching deepens our appreciation of ourselves and our life. We are freer to deal with life as it presents itself, not as we fantasize how we think it *should* be.

Self-Trust Is Required and Gained
We must trust ourselves to remain independent of external factors that try to impinge upon our personal process, freedom, and identity. We choose supportive relationships but do not rely on them or use them as props for our own insecurities. We no longer feel compelled to cling to what was once familiar. The relationship that we establish with ourselves is the foundation upon which we move to the next phase (second house and Taurus) of manifesting from our core values.

Deep Satisfaction
Self-knowing is deeply gratifying. It is very satisfying to become more self-directed and self-approving. We experience a sense of victory as we throw off the need for external validation, define our own dreams, and set and pursue our own goals.

How We Deal with Reality and Life's Challenges

I discover myself.
I don't disintegrate, disappear, or lose myself. I exist here now.
I find, define, and identify who I am.
I courageously deal with reality and my life challenges.
I lovingly accept myself.
I don't blame or criticize myself.
I claim my power, goodness, integrity, uniqueness.

I can focus on myself and my choices, and not get distracted by too many activities.
I carefully define my interests and how I choose to use my energy.

The Sequence: Moving Forward to the Second House and Taurus Territory

Realization — I am a soul living in a human body in physical reality.

Next realization — All by myself, I feel isolated and lonely. How can I survive? How can I take care of myself?

We turn to the second house of our journey and explore the Taurus archetype.

Second House/Taurus: Self-Value and Taking Care of Ourselves

The Second House and Taurus

When Saturn is in the second house, we become more present in our body and connected to physical reality. Pragmatism takes precedence. We take stock of our financial resources and investigate our priorities. What we give value to is of primary importance because our values determine what we will actually work for and manifest.

Issues and Gifts
The primary issues in the second house revolve around security, self-worth, and responsibility for self. Through our sensitivity to our body and the physical world, we learn how to survive and enjoy our physical experience.

Work Is Required
The second house requires work. There is no room for illusions about being saved by some Santa Claus or free lunch program in the second house.

Providing for ourselves requires the acquisition of money to pay for what we need, a house/apartment to live in, food, clothes, etc. A major goal in the second house is to stabilize ourselves in the physical world by being able to earn and access the necessary resources to meet our basic needs and to support our lifestyle.

We Are Our Most Valuable Resource
Our most valuable resource is ourselves. Thus, we must prioritize examining how we value ourselves, establish our self-worth, and determine what is important to us. Our search for our authentic identity in the first house expands into mining and gathering our personal resources in the second. We must uncover self-deprecating patterns that prevent us from manifesting and being nurtured in the world.

Avoid Self-Criticism, Be Self-Supportive
In the second house, we find and build the stamina, perseverance, and steadfastness to move forward on our journey. To develop the above, we must avoid self-criticism. We learn to be self-supportive and clearly evaluate what we require to move forward. If we had everything we needed in terms of both internal and external resources, traversing the second house wouldn't be necessary. This is never the case.

Physical Pleasure
The second house is not just about work. It is about enjoying our physical body, the abundance and beauty of Mother Earth, and all the gifts of human existence. Physical touching, sexual relationships, and body comforts help us establish a visceral connection with our physical body and thus prepare the ground for truly intimate relationships where we are present — not withdrawn and absent. Being present in feeling awareness in our body is also critical for creating in physical reality. We have to be here to manifest and to receive what is ours and what we earn and deserve.

Saturn and Pluto Challenges in the Second House

Taking Responsibility and Self-Honesty
Saturn in the second house can present itself as a loss of employment, money, or a relationship, which serves to wake us up to some excuse, illusion, or attachment that prevents us from taking responsibility for ourselves.

For example, we would normally choose to quit a job or relationship that we don't like or that no longer serves us before we get fired or abandoned. If we get fired or dumped before we leave voluntarily, the bottom line is always, in some way, we had abdicated responsibility and ignored the obvious signs.

We need to get honest with ourselves and reclaim our power independent of others and their values. Self-honesty is the most fundamental resource that we each must, and can, claim. It is free and the required foundation for every aspect of freedom.

Personal Value and Core Essence
Saturn and Pluto transiting or placed in the second house brings to our attention self-worth and negative self-talk. We expand our sense of self by no longer allowing ourselves to think in terms of who we "should" be and being controlled by our "roles" imposed by family or society.

We learn how to access and effectively use our inner resources to manifest physical resources. We learn how to best utilize who we are and what we have.

Getting in Touch with Self-Negating Attitudes
Saturn in Taurus and the second house press us to get in touch with the self-negating attitudes that we acquired when very young. The emotional and physical nourishment that we received, or didn't receive, when we were infants and young children determines how we perceive our value as we become adults.

These imprints in our emotional and physical bodies are attached to our psyche like glue. The healing of wounds from trauma, neglect, abuse, and abandonment requires deep self-love and acceptance, which can only come by connecting with the eternal goodness of our soul, whose value is not determined by the often traumatic and cruel encounters that humans are subjected to.

Lack and Attachment

Saturn and Pluto remind us to boldly examine what is lacking so we can honestly access what we need to do to acquire what we need. We identify and release ourselves from unnecessary and debilitating attachments and superficial needs or attempts to compensate for our neediness. We learn proper and nurturing ways to take good care of our physical body so we can be healthy and enjoy physical pleasures.

Insecurities and Basic Needs

Saturn and Pluto make us examine our primal insecurities. We get an accurate assessment of our personal and financial resources. We examine our basic needs and how we can best take care of ourselves. We learn to make distinctions between how we limit ourselves and actual limitations of time and resources. We do our best to overcome negative attitudes that are the contributing causes of "failure." We decide how to acquire and best use resources to support us on our journey. We definitely need everything that we can muster to proceed.

How We Deal with Reality and Life's Challenges

I learn how to take care of my body/health and how to support myself financially so I can meet my own needs.

I consolidate and learn to wisely use my resources.

I find courage in the face of adversity.

Self-value and honesty about what I need serve as touchstones for what works for me.

I take responsibility for myself and my life — past, present, and future.

The Sequence: Moving Forward to the Third House and Gemini Territory

As we confront limitations of time and resources, we realize that we need more information and interaction with other human beings. What else is going on in the world besides me?

Third House/Gemini: Information and Activities

The Third House and Gemini

Gemini loves activities and information. Initially, all our activities are interesting. We gather information about life as it is.

The third house is about what we notice and how we interpret what we see and hear. We learn how to interact with others and develop communication and listening skills. We grow our capacity to receive and share information in ways in which all parties feel heard and respected. Understanding, not just imparting or acquiring information, is required.

Information and Evaluation

In the third house, we explore and interact with the world outside ourselves. Initially, we indiscriminately and unconsciously gather data. Progressively, we learn to evaluate what is useful and what is excess. We also learn to discipline ourselves to not waste valuable mental space with extraneous and useless information.

We become aware of what we relate to that is not in alignment with our values. We learn how to express ourselves and acquire the intellectual foundation to establish a workable belief system from which we can navigate the world.

Our Mind and Thoughts

The third house and Gemini territory are associated with Mercury, Gemini's ruler. We learn that our mind is a powerful instrument, and we have to train it to serve instead of enslave us. We start to pay attention to how we express ourselves, use our mind, and think. We learn how to communicate, teach, and write in original and perceptive ways.

Development of Mental Skills

Because much of the information we gather directly enters our unconscious, we need to develop our capacity to discriminate, perceive what is not spoken, and become aware of misinformation.

We hone our mind and mental skills so that we can discern subtle and hidden distinctions. Listening to and trusting our intuition are critical in being able to determine what is true and valuable. We learn to identify what is a distraction and a pleasant diversion that feeds a busy mind and is satisfying only in the moment.

Experiment and Experience

The third house is a testing ground for *experiment and experience*. We should be careful not to attach the term *failure* to experiments that produce undesirable results. They simply give us valuable information. What is important is that we learn from our experiences.

Education in the World

In the third house, all our experiences, encounters, and events are educational. We interact and learn from the circumstances that present themselves and get to know ourselves better by observing how we react and interact with people and situations. We gather not only information but insights that help us organize our own ideas and communicate with more precision and clarity. We study the world around us to acquire knowledge that we can use to live a more meaningful and fruitful life.

Saturn and Pluto in the Third House and Gemini

Saturn and Pluto transiting or natally present in the third house may diminish our appreciation of our intellectual capacities, feed self-deprecating thought patterns, and spin our mind into negative mental activity. This position may also indicate learning and speaking disabilities.

Precision in Communication
Saturn and Pluto in the third house are about learning patience, precision, and careful selection in communication. We need to be understood and to understand others. We need to listen intently to others and not just focus on what we want to say next. We must take care to listen without judgment and adding our own interpretations.

Gathering the Pieces of the Map
Saturn in the third house can help us consolidate what may seem disjointed and weave information together as a map for further exploration. With patience, we can fit everything into a coherent whole. But finding a definitive solution is not necessary. We simply give value to inquisitiveness and trust that it will all make sense later. In Gemini territory, we are naturally unaware of many things because we are gathering the pieces of the puzzle which we can assemble into a coherent form later.

Developing and Trusting Our Intuition
What is important is that we cultivate our intuitive abilities so that we have a way to tune in to and discriminate what is relevant. As we develop our intuition, it connects us to deeper meaning and helps us trust what we hear when we listen. We can train ourselves to know the difference between our mental thoughts and our inner guidance. This skill requires lifelong attention and practice. It also requires knowing that guidance is not always immediate or even clear. Sometimes we just have to wait.

Family and Siblings
In Gemini territory, we discover that we are not alone. We have a family, siblings, and neighbors. There are a lot of people in our world generating a lot of activity.

The third house involves our relationships with siblings, family patterns, and placement in the family structure. Whether an only child or one of many, we each play our own role and see ourselves according to that role. When Saturn is in the third house, sharing with each other can illuminate hidden reasons for misunderstandings and clear the air.

Mental, Information, and Activity Overwhelm
Saturn and Pluto in the third house may bring feelings of overwhelm and confusion, with too much going on. We are confronted with the challenge of living in the midst of excessive activity while still meeting our own needs. We are challenged to figure out what is most relevant for us, to discriminate what is worthwhile, and to make choices.

How We Deal with Reality and Life's Challenges

To deal with my mind, I ask myself: *What am I telling myself? Am I telling myself my truth?*

I train myself to listen deeply into my physical and emotional bodies to find my truth. I listen without judgment to hear others tell their truth.

As I learn to discriminate between what is important and what is not, my perspective changes from being overwhelmed to making relevant and healthy choices.

The Sequence: Moving Forward to the Fourth House and Cancer Territory

We are unsure and ignorant of what we will find in the fourth house, but we are preparing ourselves with essential mental skills that are needed to deal with our emotional body and all its expressions. To be able to choose how we wish to dance with life, we listen to our emotions and deep feelings.

Fourth House/Cancer: Emotional Being, Inner Foundation

When any of the outer planets (Pluto, Neptune, Uranus) and Saturn cross the IC midnight point, we go deep into our inner world to discover the invisible energy and feelings that make up our being. A perceptual shift takes place. A new cycle of inner awareness begins. (See discussion of the IC in chapter 2.)

The Fourth House and Cancer Territory

The Moon is the celestial body "ruler" associated with the fourth house. In the fourth house, we get in touch with prenatal and preverbal rumblings that tell a story that we didn't even know existed. Associated with the emotions, the Cancer archetype is sensitive and defensive, feels deeply, and needs both an inner and outer home base for security. Healing in the fourth house is about releasing the past and family patterns to avoid being trapped in regrets and self-doubt. It is also about developing self-awareness through nurturing self and one's own projects.

Emotions Are Part of Our Inner-Guidance System
In the fourth house, we become starkly aware that our inner-guidance system is more complicated than thinking and listening. Intuition also has an emotional component, which can sabotage us when we don't pay attention to our instincts with our feeling sensory receptors. We expand our consciousness and our self-concept by integrating our feeling capacity into our human awareness.

Our emotions can either confine us to internal and auric fear and insecurity or help us channel our ever-moving energy into embodied feelings of aliveness. Much is hidden in our emotional body, which remains a tormenting mystery until we embrace it with self-nurturing. As we learn to self-nurture, we acquire deep satisfaction and contentment.

Midnight Mystery
The fourth house is the deep night phase of our journey, where the darkest and most mysterious parts of our psyche reside. We must reach into these hidden depths to uncover our hidden potentials. Our unconscious is most available in the fourth house. This is where we can access both demons and the Divine.

An essential part of our being will always be hidden to the world. This is a relief that reassures us that it is safe to be honest with ourselves. The important thing is that our inner reality does not remain hidden to ourselves! For it is within where we build a sense of inner security. Our successes at resolving issues from childhood (and past lives), our relationship with our parents, and tormenting memories play critical roles in achieving deep inner security. What we accomplish in the world and what we project into our outer environments are dependent upon our sense of inner-energetic connection and contentment.

Secret Wealth and Hidden Dynamics
The fourth house is the most mysterious and the source of our personal wealth. Secrets and the hidden dynamics that guide our psychological development and determine the direction of our life path are stored in the unconscious vaults of the fourth house. From an enigmatic psyche, we enter the physical world. It is from the womb of the fourth house that we build our life.

Saturn and Pluto in the Fourth House

Saturn and Pluto transiting or natally present in the fourth house creates challenges to our emotional ability to nurture and be nurtured. Fear, worry, and inner anxiety consume our emotional energy. By being in touch with our emotional body, we can cultivate feeling sensitivity and self-love, and care for and nurture ourselves.

Building an Inner Foundation
The fourth house is about building an inner foundation that connects us to our physical and emotional bodies through feeling awareness. Because our emotional body is imprinted with family patterns, this past must be revealed and dealt with to build an internal foundation that is uniquely our own. Wisely navigated, the fourth house is an ending of the old and the beginning of a new stage in our life.

Unresolved family conflicts and dysfunctional dynamics that have been deeply embedded in the subconscious must surface and be dealt with honestly. Our acknowledgement and release of deep emotional trauma and imprints clear the way for us to move less encumbered into the future. As we come to terms with family patterns, we can extricate ourselves from the rumbling chaos that pulls us into the past.

From Fear to Inner Security and Love
We are all deeply driven by our need for security and safety. Saturn and Pluto in the fourth house remind us that our task is not to be devoured by these demanding primal needs but to awaken to how we can find a peaceful sense of security within ourselves. Feeling secure is no longer about protecting ourselves from both internal and external threats; rather, it's about being bathed in a blanket of self-nurturing love.

Reclaiming Our Innocence
When the taskmaster Saturn and deep psychologist Pluto are in the fourth house, we can feel intimidated, threatened, and shamed by what we feel. But atonement and reconciliation are the goals. We are innocent and must find and accept our innocence. The human experiment was not our idea and it is not our fault! We did not enter human life and our birth, or adopted, family by conscious choice.

Door to Our Future and Destiny
Although we cannot change the past, we can change our perspective and evaluate what happened. As we deal with complex and even intimidating family patterns, we uncover the treasures of our individuality and our life path. The doors of the past open in the fourth house, but this is also where we open the door to the future.

The process of personal liberation requires separation from what has been externally imposed. The unconscious mental and emotional enmeshment must be exposed and disentangled to find and ignite the light of our soul and to retrieve the seed of our personal destiny. To walk through the door to our future, we must shed the rules and "shoulds" we acquired from our family and society and adopt our own worldview.

Healthy Separation Through Responsibility
Healthy separation is not formed from blaming others. It is formed by taking responsibility for one's own life, embracing one's uniqueness, and finding one's own internally directed self-expression. We can stop arresting our own development by eliminating misdirected rebelliousness, trying to find an easy route, or living in a fantasy world.

Our Process to Claim Our Gold
The fourth house stage of our personal process is done in secret, for we are the only ones who can discover, know, and embrace the gift of our individuality. We personally are responsible for retrieving our soul treasures. We have to face the monsters of fear and emotional intimidation to claim the gold. As we absolve our own guilt and live in gratitude, we pass through the gate of self-liberation. Ingratitude and entitlement may be less dramatic than identifiable traumatic experiences, but they too blockade the gates to the gold.

We Can Be Our Own Therapist
Unspoken truths, repressed emotions, personal and family secrets, camouflaged moods — all consume us from within. These are the demons that create our internal wars and deflect our creativity. Each one is stored in our subconscious as intertwined links in a chain waiting to be broken to free us from the prison called repression. We are the only ones who can allow these energies to be expressed in other creative and satisfying forms. We also find gifts related to our ancestors (their endurance and pioneering spirit) and current family (parents that kept up during their life challenges and put food on the table). We profit when we claim these "gifts from the garage."

To cultivate a sense of security within, we need alone time and sometimes even seclusion to connect with hidden feelings and deep sensitivity. This is not the job of a therapist. This is when we have to be our own therapist.

How We Deal with Reality and Life's Challenges

When I feel emotionally overwhelmed, I find a place of security inside myself.
I take care of myself and avoid becoming exhausted by taking care of others — to feel safe and needed.

I establish workable boundaries, not walls.
I accept that I am an emotional being. I am a woman. I am a man.
By going deep into my emotional body, I can move from feeling threatened to feeling safe inside myself.

Within, I can find a way to protect myself from being energetically used, abused, taken advantage of, which cause me to be depleted of my vital life-force energy.

I identify how I lose energy and overextend myself when trying to do everything for everybody by becoming aware of what my emotional body is doing, feeling, and communicating.

Connecting within with my feelings, I avoid being over-self-protective and building inner defenses that shut off my flow of energy.

By practicing emotional self-honesty about how I feel, I reclaim my emotional body as part of my being and use it for self-nurturing.

The Sequence: Moving Forward to the Fifth House and Leo Territory

In the fourth house, we discover that we are more than our thoughts and ideas ruminating in our mind. We become aware of the power and presence of our emotional body.

We realize there are hidden treasures within. We are ready to find self-love and our unique gifts in the fifth house and Leo territory.

Fifth House/Leo: Mining and Enjoying Our Gifts

The Fifth House and Leo Territory

We Create with Focus and Feeling
In the fifth house, we experience ourselves as not just energy, but flowing, conscious energy that is always making something happen. To direct this energy toward what we wish to create, we use mental focus, feeling awareness, and directed action.

We Shine Our Light
The Sun is the celestial planet associated with Leo and the fifth house. We shine our own light with our big heart and by sharing our unique gifts and creativity.

Self-Attention Takes Precedence
In the fifth house, self-attention and focusing on our creative endeavors take precedence. When the seeds of our gifts remain dormant, we are tormented by feelings of incompleteness. To find what is missing, we keep searching and creating to become whole. We direct our efforts toward finding the gold of self and use it to express who we are and why we are here. We nurture the seeds of our creativity into full blooming flowers.

From Raw Stone
Initially, the Leo archetype presents us with an unfashioned stone waiting to be sculpted. Lacking inspiration or support to develop our individual expressions, we can leave this stone buried or carve it in a way that does not please our heart. The fifth house helps us find the inspiration and discipline needed to shape the raw material into original and authentic expressions of love.

An Authentic Dance with Life
Home of Leo the lion-hearted, the fifth house invites us to enjoy dancing with life. Although the tone is light-hearted, there is also an undercurrent of seriousness. Our energy is not to be wasted frivolously. We must live with purpose to enjoy our life.

Saturn and Pluto in the Fifth House

When Saturn and Pluto transit or are natally located in the fifth house, we devote our attention to discovering the treasures hidden within. From the feeling space of our essence that we got in touch with in the fourth house, we now explore how we can bring our talents into physical form.

Illusions of Love Cause Frustration
Saturn and Pluto expose egocentric tendencies, misuses of power, and dramas that we create to get attention. When our standards for success and relationships are based on illusions, Saturn and Pluto in the fifth house can make us feel frustrated and depressed. We cannot be happy living with false notions and fairytale thinking. Saturn's realism helps us break these sabotaging patterns. Pluto makes sure we become aware of our own insecurities, illusions, and beliefs around being able to give and receive love.

Mirroring Our Fears and Fantasies
Saturn and Pluto create a mirror that reflects our egotistical tendencies, revealing our worst fears. If we are willing to take an unflinching look, we can get in touch with how we hold ourselves captive, suppressed by our fears, deluded by our fantasies, falsely protected by blame, and willfully avoiding responsibility for our own inner reality.

Our Heart Becomes Our Guide
To productively use Saturn and Pluto in the fifth house, we search for insight into how to connect with the love within so we can attract it from without. Saturn and Pluto help us find our way back to our heart.

In the fifth house, we discover humble self-love and learn to listen to our heart as a guide to what we create and attract. We learn that only that which is directed by and aligned with our heart is truly satisfying and a source of joy.

Saturn and Pluto require that we draw on our deep, heart-felt attention to access our talents and gifts and to find our life purpose. How we choose to use our energy and what we choose to create are integral parts of self-discovery and self-realization. Whatever path we follow and creative endeavors we pursue, they must lead to a deep sense of contentment and love, which we find only in our heart.

Slow Manifesting Force
The presence of Saturn and Pluto in the fifth house can feel like an impeding force that restricts our creative flow. But we must remember that the earth energy of Saturn is about manifestation. We cannot bring into being anything without Saturn's assistance.

Taking Responsibility
Saturn and Pluto remind us that taking responsibility for what we create is a central theme in the fifth house. The treasures that we are ultimately looking for, must refine, and bring into manifestation are our personal expressions of love.

Protecting the Heart
Although sexual passion is part of the fifth house dynamic, all expressions of love must be deepened to endure. Any relationships that are abusive or threaten further awakening of the heart produce restrictions and burdens that must be cast off. Saturn and Pluto are very protective of our heart and what we let in and share.

The Unfolding Process of Creation
Self-expression is key in the fifth house. We must believe in and invest in ourselves. Expecting to quickly produce an idealized version of what we want to create can prevent us from engaging in the unfolding process of creation and manifesting. For example, books have many drafts and editions. Artwork starts with sketches. We must be present to all phases of the creative process.

Enjoying Creating from Within
Saturn and Pluto push us to get in touch with how we create from within. At the same time, Leo wants us to have fun digging for our hidden treasures and expressing our talents. As we learn to identify what pulls us away from our heart, we get in touch with our inner guru. As we let go of what diminishes our light, we become radiant beings. As we avoid wasting our energy on superficial affairs and endeavors, we learn to enjoy life. We channel our emotions to healing and regeneration through our creativity.

How We Deal with Reality and Life's Challenges

I open my heart to myself. I get in touch with my gifts.

Everything in my life is a joyful creation.

I enjoy being warm, enthusiastic, dramatic, and affectionate. Every day in every way, I play, sing, dance, and have fun.

I play the game of life with a sense of trust and ease.
Offering the gifts of my soul, I shine my light and am recognized and appreciated for who I am.

The Sequence: Moving into the Sixth House and Virgo Territory

At the end of our journey through the fifth house, we realize that we can be too self-centered and self-absorbed. How can we find independence and live from our radiance and wholeness in jobs and situations that require our interaction with others? We are ready to step into the world in the sixth house.

Sixth House/Virgo: Consolidate an Independent Self

The Sixth House and Virgo

The sixth house is about consolidating ourselves and our identity while adjusting to different environments. In the process of taking care of mundane activities, we perfect skills, learn how to be present to details, and digest our previous experiences into useful strategies. We organize our personal resources into their most useful form.

Transition House
In the transition houses (third, sixth, ninth, and twelfth), our job is to learn to pay attention to everyday events and the details of making life work. It is easy to fall into routines, responses, and habits that mechanize instead of bring awareness and precision to details. The more we lapse into unconscious behavior, the less prepared we are to effectively and creatively interact in the world.

Preparing Ourselves
We may feel restless and yearn for more interactions and activity. The present may seem boring. If so, we can productively use the time to learn new skills, refine and update old ones, and to take better care of ourselves. We can prepare ourselves for an unknown future by cleaning up and clearing out both our physical space and our body. In terms of employment, we need to focus on what we are learning that can prepare us for advancement or a career change in the future.

Creating Good Habits
One of the best uses of Virgo energy is to create good habits. This doesn't sound very exciting or glamorous, but good habits are the foundation of a good life and powerful projection. Paying attention to our habitual behavior and making choices that serve our well-being are the basis of taking responsibility for our life. As we pay attention to, monitor, and streamline how we do things, we become more and more self-directed, efficient, and effective.

Cultivate Skills, Humility, and Gratitude
In the sixth house, we get very clear about and hone our talents, skills, gifts, and interests. We must avoid being too critical and judgmental of self and others. Instead of focusing on imperfections, indulging in self-doubt, and being overwhelmed by details, we need to search for deeper meaning in the mundane and live modestly with humility and gratitude for life.

Saturn and Pluto in the Sixth House

What We Can Control and What We Can't
When Saturn and Pluto are in the sixth house, we are prodded to learn how to deal with the demands and challenges over which we have little or no control. We are presented with opportunities that teach us the three indispensable life skills described in the Serenity Prayer: (1) taking care of what we can control, (2) letting go of what we can't control, and (3) creating boundaries and guidelines that help us tell the difference.

Trust the Process
Saturn and Pluto encourage us to work with and trust the process that is allowing us to consolidate our inner resources and to embody our presence so it can work for us in the next stages of our life. These are subtle but critical skills that will have practical applications in our ability to manifest and succeed in the world.

Burned Out? Take Care of Your Health
When Saturn and Pluto are in the sixth house, we can feel burned out or exhausted. These are serious signs that it is time to pull back and take care of our health. Loss of employment, illness, or other "surprises" are simply a way to get our attention and to force us to take care of what we have neglected (ourselves) and denied (our sensitivity and own needs).

It is often only under duress that we wake up, pay attention, and finally get honest with ourselves. This can be a perfect time to change our lifestyle, including adopting healthier food regimes and physical exercise routines. Discipline and commitment are key to consolidating and caring for ourselves so that we can more effectively deal with life. Practical adjustments serve a greater purpose in helping us prepare to handle the logistics of daily living as well as to develop the inner strength to deal with a more complicated existence in the future.

Let Go and Let Life Unfold
The sixth house is where we prepare ourselves by releasing bad habits and attachments. We are well advised to choose what is useful and leave the rest behind.

We must become conscious of our internal dialogue, stories, and projections that we are taking into relationships and into the world. Also, if self-care has been superseded by attention to others and circumstances, we need to shift our priorities back to ourselves. We train ourselves to not lose ourselves in the process of dealing with complicated and demanding interactions.

Consolidate and Prepare
Our overall challenge in Virgo territory and the sixth house is to consolidate our beingness and skills that prepare us to move into the outer world. Building our self-confidence is an important part of our preparation, which helps us release the Virgo tendency of trying to be perfect.

How We Deal with Reality and Life's Challenges

I redefine perfect as *what is* and accept life as it unfolds.
I am capable of operating in the world. I consolidate my skills and my identity.
I am not emotionally attached or dependent in relationships.

I can be happy separate and alone.

I serve without servitude and make my own decisions about what I want to do and give. Consolidated within myself, I am self-satisfied and whole.

The Sequence: Moving into the Seventh House and Libra Territory

We realize that we need interaction with others. We are ready to step into the seventh house and explore the fascinating world of personal relationships.

Seventh House/Libra: Personal Relationships

When any of the outer planets (Pluto, Neptune, Uranus) and Saturn cross the descendant, we enter into an expanded world that includes personal relationships. We are no longer alone. Our new reality demands a perceptual shift that not only includes others but *how we are in relationship with others*. The training wheels are off our bicycle. Our life and priorities get rearranged. (See the discussion of the descendant in chapter 2.)

The Pivotal Role of Relationships

How and why we relate to and interact with others are determining factors that affect every aspect of our life and are the foundation for all the subsequent steps on our journey: intimate partnership (eighth house), spiritual advancement (ninth house), worldly success (tenth house), community (eleventh house), and our relationship with a higher power (twelfth house).

Whether Saturn and Pluto in Capricorn fall in your seventh house or not, we all need to optimize our interactions, because if we come unhinged in relationships, everything else falls apart.

We live in a sea of relationships. We are always interacting with other people, situations, worldly circumstances, and cosmic forces. We are in relationship with the weather, noises, ever-changing environments, and energies and information that we can't even identify. We are in relationship with time and divine timing, with our bodies, emotions, mind, and our own rhythms. Everything is in relationship to everything else. We are never alone. We are dependent upon relationships. Relationships give us value, pleasure, support, *and* problems.

With both Saturn and Pluto in the seventh house, we investigate the all-inclusive deep dynamics of "me" in relationship. Our level of peace or stress depends on how we relate and interact in all types of relationships. In the seventh house, our laboratory is personal relationships — intimate, familial, and with close friends. The eleventh house is about relationships within a group dynamic — friends on a shared mission.

The Seventh House and Libra

The Challenges
Our challenges in the seventh house and Libra territory focus on social interactions and feelings of being accepted, rejected, or loved. We learn how to interact, cultivating the skills of being present, kind, and nonjudgmental. To do so, we have to work on releasing delusions, expectations, and control trips. We learn about compromise, fairness, empathy, and diplomacy.

Emotional Enmeshment and Distinctions
Relationships are the territory where we learn to make distinctions between ourselves and others. We learn about the human condition of emotional enmeshment and also the human challenge of staying connected without entangling ourselves energetically. We must address the underlying causes of enmeshment, including neediness, low self-esteem, and a lack of completeness within ourselves.

Boundaries, Accountability, and Obligations
In relationship, we make choices that impact both ourselves and others. We learn about being accountable to ourselves and others. We learn how to distinguish between what is an obligation and what is not. We learn about compromise and accepting change.

Independent and Honest
If we have made progress in self-definition and achieved a comfortable degree of independence in Virgo territory (and in all the first six houses), we can be honest without creating needless drama to get attention or to try to be right. Being honest with others can happen only when we are able to be honest with ourselves.

Saturn and Pluto in the Seventh House

Saturn and Pluto in the seventh house challenge us to seriously examine how we live in the interactive arena where boundaries, differentiation, and respect are required. We gain clarity about personal responsibility — ours and others'.

Fantasies and Projections Take a Reality Test
Saturn and Pluto are tough teachers in the seventh house, where they expose our attachment to relationship fantasies. We have to learn to be clear and not muddy the waters with hopeful fantasies that somehow the other will change to make things work out.

The way we deal with ourselves shifts when we are in relationship with other human beings. Above the horizon (houses 7-12), we must become aware of what we project and evaluate the extent to which our projections (including wishful thinking) reflect actual experience and reality. Illusions of ideal relationships are put to the reality test. We are initiated into a new way of being that demands being real and realistic.

Acceptable and Compatible
Saturn and Pluto test the grounds of compatibility, which hinge on what is acceptable for each individual and where we can comfortably accommodate. We learn to honestly identify what is intolerable and to not make excuses. Patterns of relating based on domination, control, power

over, submission, and inequality are not okay.

Can We Stand Alone and Together in Relationships?
Only in actual encounters are we able to undergo the tests we face in relationships. The principal test is whether we can stand alone and be authentic with ourselves and each other. This requires being able to be both separate and together as individuals. When we can both differentiate and flow together, we can find independence and harmony in relationships. And we can experience the many dimensions of love!

Yogi Bhajan once said, "Life is a game, but we do not want to play unattached. We want to play for the sake of winning and losing, and that is where unhappiness comes in." Our goal is to learn to play unattached for the sake of enjoying each other and our lives together. That is where happiness comes in.

The Search for Connection and What Gets in the Way
What we are searching for in relationships is connection. To cultivate deep connection, Pluto in the seventh house helps us look at what is getting in the way. By paying attention to the nature of our interactions and how we react and respond, our relationships give us feedback that helps us get in touch with our relationship with ourselves. The more we learn about ourselves, the more we can learn about and connect with others.

The most basic thing to observe is how we respond internally (mentally and emotionally) when interacting with others: (1) Do I feel safe or threatened? (2) Can I stay present or do I space out to avoid feeling uncomfortable, or cower in fear? (3) Am I defensive or can I listen without judgment and interpretation based on what I want?

Fear- and anger-based reactions indicate that we feel overwhelmed and can't handle the situation. We don't feel safe, accepted, understood, listened to, or loved. We may rightly feel that our emotional, physical, and mental boundaries are being violated. We may also feel that we do not have adequate boundaries to defend or protect ourselves, or exit an abusive situation.

Saturn and Pluto teach us to be present to our responses in both challenging and harmonious situations. Where we are triggered and react helps us identify our issues and programs, which helps us take responsibility and cease to blame others.[27]

Pluto Reveals Deep Issues
Pluto in the seventh house will inevitably bring us face-to-face with our own issues.

Self-Acceptance and Self-Love
How we view and interact in all our relationships is based on our relationship with ourselves,

---

[27] Nonviolent communication (NVC) was formulated by a Libra, Marshall Rosenberg. NVC is a communication system that sets out ways to talk to each other so that neither party feels like they are being attacked, thus triggering defensive responses.

which is a function of self-knowing, self-acceptance, and self-love. Neediness is a result of feeling empty and a desire to fill an emotional void created by lack of connection with self. If we feel depressed and lost, we have not yet established a compassionate relationship with our soul self. Believing that we are not good enough seeds jealously, the need for approval, and the fear of not being accepted and loved. We hide behind masks that separate us from both ourselves and others.

Boundaries
Whether we are controlled by and a victim of others' behavior or dominate relationships with manipulation and power-over control tactics, we lack mature energetic boundaries. The unhealthy state of codependence is a function of being unable to separate ourselves from others and emotional enmeshment.

Relationship Addictions
Reactive behavior is a mild to serious form of addiction. Something or someone seems to control our behavior. Addicts feel powerless over their addictions because their reptilian brain is in charge of their behavior. The reptilian brain is the human survival mechanism — fight or flight. When the reptilian brain is in charge, we can't be present to and make choices from the rational mind (midbrain). And without the neutral mind, which is activated in the frontal lobe of the brain, the rational/dualistic mind becomes conflictual and is controlled by the subconscious mind or reptilian brain. We know our reptilian brain is dominating when we hold on or can't let go or disengage from old stories and responses.

Harmony and Peace in Neutral

Saturn and Pluto in the seventh house create circumstances that make us realize the necessity of connecting with our neutral mind so that we can find our own balance, peace, and equilibrium, and remain in that state while interacting with others.

The Libra scales are balanced only in the neutral meditative mind. The ability to access and operate from our neutral mind determines our ability to (1) establish and maintain boundaries, (2) stay calm and not react (at least not overreact), (3) not take what others say personally, and (4) separate from and observe what is outside ourselves.

When we are not directed from our own center and our actions are focused on responding to and accommodating external cues, we will be reactive, defensive, or submissive; that is, be controlled by others and circumstances. External triggers activate the reptilian brain. We are preoccupied with *What I think you think about me* and *What you are doing to me*.

The Powers of the Neutral Mind

In sum, dealing with relationship issues requires working out conflicts within ourselves first, which we do by taking ourselves out of our reptilian brain and observing with our neutral mind. Access to our neutral mind gives us the power to

- ♦ Accept, understand, listen without judgment

- Separate our own energy and identity from others
- Observe without emotional and mental entanglement
- Move out of mentally and emotionally conflicted and reactive states
- Disengage and distance ourselves from the fray
- Be at peace within and cease to engage in or project aggressive attitudes
- Be self-sufficient and content with ourselves and not needy or dependent on others
- Cease to blame others and take responsibility for our own behavior

Yogi Bhajan shared that a wise and spiritual person is the one who is neutral in a relationship.

Relationships Are a Journey to the Heart

Especially with Saturn and Pluto, there is always a level of stress in relationships, which can diminish to an interactive dance when we find a common interface and alignment in the heart space of higher soul love.

We can take advantage of Saturn and Pluto in the seventh house to learn how to let love in, to receive and not block an energetic flow between others and ourselves. By observing and feeling where we block and resist connection by distracting ourselves from the present moment, we can train ourselves to be present in feeling awareness and avoid escaping into our mind with disconnected talking and analysis. We open the door to our own heart by releasing fear, anger, and beliefs that close the heart and by training ourselves to receive what is already there.

Libra and its ruling planet Venus teach us that relationships are a journey to the heart, where we are actually capable of experiencing connected unconditional love. Saturn and Pluto in the seventh house show us what makes this possible. They certainly do not support relationship fantasies, but they do teach us what we have to do to prepare ourselves for deep meaningful connections. They may not offer us a joyride, but they give us the perseverance to learn what we need to learn to have what our soul yearns for. These long-term planets stick with us and support us in growing up and waking up to love.

With Saturn and Pluto in the seventh house, we can build a foundation in the neutral channel in our mind that makes it possible to interact with give and take, compassion, and acceptance of what we cannot control. It takes work to cultivate and maintain neutral consciousness, but if we desire intimacy, sincerity, honesty, authenticity, closeness, and unconditional love, we better do what it takes to live in our neutral heart/mind. It is actually blissful to be in a state where we accept others and things the way they are and preferences and opinions don't get in the way of the heart connection that we are seeking.

How We Deal with Reality and Life's Challenges

I can wisely choose those I wish to establish relationships with.
I can be compassionate and detached. I do not need to take care of or fix anyone.
I can honestly be myself and let others be so too.

I no longer operate from the hope that someone else can "save me."

I accept people the way they are, not how I want them to be or think they should be.
I can stay neutral and listen without defensiveness, judgments, or trying to be right.
In my communications, I seek to understand and accept others while I stay present to my own feelings and needs.

The Sequence

Everything changes and evolves in relationships. We are working toward our exploration of the eighth house where individualization and flow are prerequisites. We are ready to interact and create in deep intimacy because we have found alignment between equals who have found and operate from wholeness within themselves. We are ready to use the power of love to empower our creative endeavors.

Eighth House/Scorpio: Cycles, Death, and Rebirth

The eighth house is ruled by Pluto. Any planets in the eighth house are always subject to Pluto's influence. When Saturn and Pluto reside in or transit the eighth house, their energies and lessons are intensified.

The Eighth House and Scorpio

Scorpio and the eighth house are about completion, renewal, regeneration, and freedom — themes that infuse all areas of life.

The eighth house is about perpetual metamorphosis and the cycles of life, death, and rebirth. We do not physically die, but something is purged to make space for an expanded expression of self. Chaos is followed by the restoration of order at a higher level of being. And the cycle continues.

There is always another round of being and becoming. We identify where we were, where we are now, and allow ourselves to become a deeper and more conscious version of what we have always been: a radiant soul exploring physical reality.

Alchemy Through Collaboration

The eighth house is about the alchemy of the soul through the elevation of opposites into complements. Interaction with others in some form is part of the process. Through intimate, professional, or other cooperative partnerships, our collaboration ignites another level of consciousness and creates something that we could not create alone.

Inner Alchemy in Relationships
In the eighth house, sexuality and relationships have deeper meaning and transcendent purpose. The goal of bonding is to consummate inner alchemy.

Opposites Confront to Transform
Opposites confront each other, not to fight or to conquer, but to force each other to submit to existential transformation.

A tortured dualistic inner world rises to the surface in dramatic and possibly even life-threatening situations. Mixed messages, contradictory actions, and duplicitous attitudes precipitate both inner and outer crises. Transformation is the only viable option. It is imposed, demanded, and required.

A new status and deeper understanding restore balance in the situation.

Superficiality Is Not Accepted

We cannot live a superficial life and get away with it in the eighth house. The image of ourselves that we project cannot be phony. Delusional definitions of relationships are not permitted. We cannot continue to live behind superficial masks. Any form of camouflage is exposed and rendered useless.

Saturn and Pluto in the Eighth House

The following themes are part of the eighth house and Scorpio process. They are intensified when Saturn and Pluto are in our eighth house.

Examine Motives
Saturn and Pluto transits through and presence in the eighth house caution us to examine the motives and sincerity of all partners. Commitment is required. There is nothing casual or temporary about Scorpio and Pluto. Partnership in crime can also happen in the eighth house. There are always motivations to be uncovered and lessons to learn.

Integrity Is Built into Scorpio – Examples
I was talking to a Scorpio friend who was an ambassador. He told me that people asked him all the time to do unethical things. He always said no. Then he added, if this got out of control, he would quit rather than compromise his principles.

I also know a Scorpio real estate agent. When the banks promoted unsustainable loans for the purchase of houses, he never allowed any of his clients to take one of those loans. When the bubble burst in the financial credit market, none of his clients lost their houses in foreclosure.

Breaking from the Past to Be Reborn
What is important about the events that confront us is how we deal with them. Depth, integrity, and brutal honesty are required. No superficiality or unethical cheating is allowed.

We undergo a metamorphosis that marks a break from what went before. Death in the eighth house means that we truly leave the past behind. We have to die (detach from the past) in order to be reborn. We leave behind our most consuming fears, which live in our unconscious. We must be conscious to release ourselves from their subversive influence.

Death of the Ego
Death of the ego, leading to an even deeper level of rebirth, refers to the process of letting go of an unconscious identity structure so that it can be replaced by a more conscious identity that is able to listen to and follow our heart and not be controlled by our fears and childish programming.

Our Relationship with Money
Our relationship with money and wealth earned through business and partnerships is an eighth house issue. Our goal is not only financial freedom, but emotional freedom in how we deal with money, finances, and the power that accompanies wealth, or the lack of power that comes with insufficient resources and poverty.

Dealing with Our Emotional History

In the eighth house, we continue to deal with the emotions brought up in the fourth house. Our whole being is tethered to our emotional history and unresolved traumas and misunderstandings. We need to probe deeply to uncover how our interpretations of childhood events formed our reactive patterns and motivations to protect ourselves. Liberation is possible only when we release the conditioned imprints that create inner conflict. The essence of the death-rebirth process is to transcend to a deeper level of inner peace.

Pressure to Change
In the eighth house and Scorpio territory, we deal with the past and the pressure to change and adapt to an ever-changing world inside and out. We are prodded to pay close attention to what is transpiring with our inner-emotional reality. We must identify what tethers us to the past, controls our psyche, destroys our peace of mind, and sabotages our life.

Saturn and Pluto in the eighth house intensify the demands for dealing with deep anger, frustration, festering resentments, and the tendency to try to control and manipulate to get what we want. There are inner and outer power struggles, and much happens in secrecy. Getting in touch with the above makes it possible to access and effectively use our deep intuitive wisdom.

How We Deal with Reality and Life's Challenges

I recognize life is a continuous cycle of death, rebirth, and meaningful living.
I am always in the process of cleansing and elevating how I deal with life and myself.
The process is never over, but I get better at handling myself and my life.
I am committed and determined to go deeper to more harmoniously and effectively accept and move through the cycles of life.
I know that I must continuously let go to move forward and not stay stuck.

The Sequence

This is all very heavy. But with a higher perspective, we can bring some light into this darkness. Our desire to identify an elevated perspective leads us into the ninth house.

Ninth House/Sagittarius: Higher Detached Perspective

The ninth house is where we awaken the higher mind and acquire a more comprehensive perspective of life and its mysteries. The ninth house is less restrictive than the eighth, and we welcome a more expansive environment.

The Ninth House and Sagittarius Territory

We can enjoy a lightness of being and optimistic approach to life in the ninth house, which is associated with Jupiter, the ruler of Sagittarius.

A Spiritual Understanding of Life
In the third house, we gathered information. In the sixth house, we assimilated and organized useful information into a practical approach to dealing with life. In the ninth house, we move beyond factual information to a spiritual understanding of what life is about.

Uncovering Limited Belief Systems
From the ninth house higher perspective, we can reflect on all our experiences so far and uncover the belief system or paradigm from which we operate. We notice the recurrent themes in the story that we tell ourselves and others. We realize that we are living our life from this story.

We Need a Broader Perspective
We need a broader, more inclusive perspective to operate more effectively in the world. The heavy seriousness in Scorpio territory can confine us to perpetual processing to extricate ourselves from our emotional underworld. In the ninth house, we get a break. Actually, there are no breaks, but in the ninth house, with the optimism of Sagittarius and Jupiter, we can feel lighter, hopeful, encouraged.

We realize that in order to not backslide and recreate our past, we need a new operating mode, a more expansive and inclusive operating system. We need to direct our attention to the present and the future instead of the past. We are driven to look at our belief system, which determines how we interpret our life experiences.

An Exit from Duality
In the ninth house, we awaken our higher mind that liberates us from conflictual duality. We discover an exit from duality and a portal to unity.

We awaken our intuition and train ourselves to listen to it, and in the process, we learn not to pay heed to our inner chatter.

Saturn and Pluto in the Ninth House

Waking Up Is Critical
When Saturn transits or occupies the ninth house, we take our spiritual path and awakening process seriously. We understand the importance of waking up and staying awake. For without

the higher mind, we will forever be pulled back into dualistic thinking and inner torment.

Signs of Duality and Limited Ego
Saturn and Pluto can feed cynicism, hopelessness, and depression, which are signs that we have not yet awakened to a reality beyond our limiting ego. Our mind is still operating in the dualistic channel, causing confusion and discontent. We are still attached to and controlled by dualistic thinking and believe that we can figure things out. We are caged in analysis paralysis.

Finding Meaning and Purpose, Freedom from Beliefs and Dogma
Spiritual and philosophical education is a dominant theme in the ninth house. Exploration of the meaning and purpose of life is the driving force. With Saturn and Pluto in the ninth house, we are challenged to overcome tendencies of the dualistic mind to fixate our attention on "beliefs" instead of experiences. A serious pitfall is getting caught up in righteous, idealized, and dogmatic beliefs. We can get enmeshed in dogmas that control our mind instead of cultivating experiences that free the mind from orthodoxy and dogmas.

Experience of a Higher Power
Saturn and Pluto allow no "false gods." We must open ourselves to our personal experience of a higher power, which can deliver us to trust and surrender to a power greater than ourselves, of which we are a part. Attitudes must be replaced with visceral experiences of our personal relationship with the Divine.

From Limitations to Wisdom
Saturn and Pluto in the ninth house expose why we feel limited — because we lack the wisdom that is gained through knowledge, which is gained through experience. Saturn and Pluto present us with life situations that demand a higher perspective, which opens us to allowing our life experiences to be directed by our intuition, heart, and spiritual wisdom. The Saturn and Pluto process culminates in internalized wisdom.

The Ninth House Process
The challenges in our ninth house revolve around being aware of the belief system from which we operate and then expanding our view and interpretation of life. We are able to release the past with a higher and more inclusive perspective of life.

Our time with Saturn and Pluto in the ninth house introduces us to another way of life. Themes include adventure, freedom, expansion, meaning, and purpose. With insight and wisdom, we become agents of change. We practice what we preach and become teachers to help others awaken to their truth.

A Contract with Our Soul
In the ninth house, we enter into a contract with our soul. Actually, we become aware of our soul contract for this lifetime. We take responsibility for ourselves as part of a greater whole, both planetary and universal. We use our higher neutral mind to engage in the next phases of our journey.

How We Deal with Reality and Life's Challenges

I can be neutral and speak for myself from my own truth.
An existential shift within me results in a deep transformation.
I no longer attach myself to the past.
The present is where I create and expand into the future.
I am a spiritual being on a spiritual mission to serve my soul.

The Sequence

Using the Sagittarius centaur as our guide, we keep our feet on the ground and seek to apply what we learn in the world.

As we develop faith in ourselves, and in our belief/experience that our life and destiny are directed by our soul and a higher power, we eagerly move into the real world of the tenth house.

Tenth House/Capricorn: We Are Tested in the World

The Midheaven Is a New Game

As discussed in chapter 8, the midheaven (MC) moves us into the final phases of our life (houses 10–12) where we deal with career matters, social integration, and finally spiritual connection. We refine our sense of identity and individuality through our professional and social accomplishments and become an authority in our own way.

Saturn and Pluto MC transits can bring a change in life direction, reputation, and more fulfillment in the world. We get more clarity about our life path and make serious career decisions.

The Tenth House and Capricorn Territory

In the tenth house, we begin a new phase of experimentation. Different hopes and aspirations related to identity, career, lifestyle, status, personal authority in the world, and positions of power become our focus. We uncover our life purpose and make a commitment to ourselves to direct our life toward making our contribution.

We enter uncharted territory in the tenth house, heading off in unexplored directions and forging a new path. We meet both our fate and our destiny. Our sense of social responsibility is fully activated.

Initiative and Experimentation
As a cardinal house, the tenth is where we are driven to take initiative. We must be flexible because we are experimenting and testing our ideas of what we want to accomplish and whom we want to be in the world. We discover latent gifts as we encounter new challenges. But with so much going on that is beyond our control, we learn to focus on what we can control: our

own moods, actions, and goals.

We allow the tenth house to work for us when we give ourselves credit for simply trying and being present to the interactive dynamics as they present themselves. It is easier to avoid insecurities and maintain an adventurous attitude when we keep in mind that we are in unknown territory and that we are participating in both discovering and creating an expanded reality in our life.

Saturn and Pluto in the Tenth House and Capricorn Territory

The following themes are part of the tenth house and Capricorn process. They are intensified when Saturn and Pluto are in our tenth house.

Alone in Public
In the tenth house, we become aware of the extent to which we are responsible for our own life and that we must develop confidence in our own authority. An additional feature of the tenth house is visibility. Our actions are public. We are on stage. There is no place to hide. We cannot revert back to our mother's womb and comforting embrace.

Saturn and Pluto invite us to revisit our early imprints of loss, abandonment, and abuse that we can unconsciously project into the world. We return to the fourth house to look at family patterns that influence our motives, ambition, and aspirations.

Our Emotional Maturity Is Challenged
Our sense of inner security is challenged, and our fourth and eighth house emotional development is tested in the outer world. This is the time when our highest aspirations come into play. We will never know what we are capable of if we don't enter the game. In the process of being in the game, we will gain self-confidence and a level of self-mastery that is available only when we participate fully.

Ready to Be Tested
Self-focus and self-discipline are required in the tenth house. We cannot predict or control the moves by the other players. We must be present and ready to respond to unpredictable and unintelligible circumstances. A driving force within and a yet-unexpressed potential yearns to be potentized.

Evaluation of Our Performance
We are inevitably evaluated by society. It is tricky business in a world that is not necessarily structured around ethical values and the highest good for each individual and for the whole community. Our status may be determined according to our willingness to fit in and to abandon our own values.

The tenth house teaches us to continuously evaluate our performance by our own standards and ethics. We must hold firm to our own values while adjusting to what is best for the whole. Should we give priority to material gain? Maybe we can have status and material gain without taking advantage of others and not compromising ourselves in the process. This is what we have to figure out for ourselves.

Tested in the Game
This is the territory where we both win and lose. There are both impediments and facilitators. We are both tested and offered gifts. Winning is about staying present to the game and mastering strategies that keep us playing.

We become acutely aware of consequences as we make choices about what to include and what to exclude in our life.

Responsibility and Sustainability
Whatever we want and work for must be backed up by taking responsibility for our choices, and what we encounter must be within our control to influence.

It is important to not let our enthusiasm create an overload which we are unable to sustain. Fortunately, Saturn reminds us to be realistic and to take stock of what we can manage. Pluto reminds us to act with integrity.

Authentic Relationship with Self
In Capricorn territory, our relationship with self must be solid and authentic. We cannot hide behind a false external persona. Whatever is out of integrity must be examined and will be exposed.

Tested by Our Own Values
The tenth house is full of tests. The ideals we hold dear will be tested. Can we maintain the ethical standards we have set for ourselves? Can we withstand the examination and critique of our actions and continue to believe in ourselves and our mission?

In the ninth house, we explored our worldview and defined the ethical standards by which we are committed to live our life. In the tenth house, we are tested by our own standards. We have to learn to trust our own integrity and live in our own truth. Re-evaluation and choices will be made with our personal truth as the foundation.

In the big world of organizations, structures, and competing egos, we have to adjust to the practical demands of the world. We have to learn how to discriminate between what works for us and what doesn't; what we can trust and what we can't.

The biggest tests in the tenth house are to be honest with ourselves and take responsibility for our choices. Saturn and Pluto require re-evaluation of our life purpose and direction. We rid ourselves of delusional beliefs. As we interact in the world, we grow; we realize what beliefs are dogmatic and thus not authentic.

Evaluating Our Success
Evaluation of our success in the world will depend upon our criteria for success. Actually, our ultimate success will depend on our ability to align with the mission of our soul. We are both supported and confronted by an inner knowing that steers our course. We question and

redefine our goals, motives, and values many times. We become aware of fears that generate feelings of inadequacy, self-doubt, and self-criticism. We move forward, overcome fears, and gain self-confidence. Yogi Bhajan told us, "It is not the life that matters; it is the courage that you bring to it."

Who Am I in the World?

Saturn and Pluto in the tenth house challenge us to figure out who we are in the world. We claim the right to our own journey, not someone else's. We learn about claiming our own authority, misuses of authority, appropriate and inappropriate ambition, status, and fame. We learn to deal with worldly power dynamics, navigating power structures, and issues related to productivity, achievement, and respect.

Over time, being recognized by others diminishes in importance. What is important is that we recognize ourselves!

How We Deal with Reality and Life's Challenges

I operate in the world from my own standards and integrity.
I take responsibility for my choices and their consequences.

I recognize myself in the world.

I take time to create a sense of inner security that I take into the world.
I meet my challenges with courage and confidence in myself.

The Sequence

In the tenth house, we learn to deal with the present as we both prepare for and create our future. At some point, we become less enamored with status and success and start to shift our focus to the contribution we can make by joining with like-minded souls. We want more than the status quo. We want to contribute to transforming the world.

Eleventh House/Aquarius: How We Create Together

The Eleventh House and Aquarius

Aquarius and its ruler Uranus are the archetypes that represent the offbeat, unusual, and even strange aspects of our humanness. Those with these energies must accept their unique nature and the fact that they may not fit into the status quo. In order to not feel marginalized or go adrift, they must live their lives with authentic passion and meaning. Those with an Aquarian disposition and motivations are not content until they have made their contribution to the collective or their community.

Social Integration

The tenth and eleventh houses are about social integration — how we as individuals fit in, interact, contribute, and use shared resources. We benefit personally from our efforts when what we add is computed as adding value to the whole.

In the tenth house, we challenge our personal status quo. In the eleventh house, we work together to challenge the collective status quo.

Aligning with a Group
Group consciousness is the force to be reckoned with in the eleventh house. A primary challenge in the eleventh is to align ourselves with a group. A problem that many face is that there has to be a friendly group to align with.

In Aquarian territory, it can be difficult to connect in community and integrate into society. When we perceive society and its institutions as hostile to what we stand for, we experience alienation, social rejection, and aloneness.

In the eleventh house, we are linked to the group collective and collective consciousness. It is through participation in an organization that we become responsible members of our community.

Relationships Are Critical
Our social influence depends upon our relationships with others and our position in the group dynamic. It is in relation to others that our position and status are defined and our influence is determined.

It is always difficult to organize and manage collective enterprises made up of so many ego-directed individuals. Some don't want to fit in. Some can't fit in. Some try and are reduced to anonymity. And of course, some get along just fine.

Our accountability shifts from ourselves to the group of which we are a part. How we interact and the role we play are exposed to public examination.

Desire to Make Our Contribution
In the eleventh house, we must choose how we wish to use our resources, gifts, and energy to contribute to the collective. Our need for approval and recognition in the tenth house is superseded by our desire to serve. It is our selfless offering that is recognized, as was the case with figures like Mahatma Gandhi, Martin Luther King Jr., and Nelson Mandela.

Larger Than Ourselves
Our participation in the collective reflects our desire to be part of something larger than ourselves. The nature of our participation will simultaneously contribute to forming the collective and defining its values and goals. Our search for meaning is bound up with the group of which we are a part. At this stage, we must be able to find and maintain our individual identity and define our unique contribution in order to flow harmoniously with the composite group dynamic. We join together, work together, create together. We need each other. Optimally, everyone shines and is important.

Saturn and Pluto in the Eleventh House

When Saturn and Pluto enter or are natally in our eleventh house, we are drawn to social activism and responsibility and finding like-minded friends with whom we can work on shared concerns.

Saturn in the eleventh house is on fairly stable ground if we have undergone deep inner and outer scrutiny in the tenth house. If we have been true to our values and acted in integrity with our heart, we have an increased sense of independence and inner authority upon which effective interaction and the ability to move forward are based.

The presence of Pluto is, however, problematic because there is always more truth to uncover. Pluto will expose where we have compromised our values and taken advantage of our position and power to exploit situations for our own profit.

The eleventh house can be uncomfortable territory because we reap what we have sown in the tenth. Those who steadfastly maintain their limited ego identity selfishly refined in the tenth house open themselves to unpleasant surprises in the eleventh house. We either receive love or retribution in the eleventh house.

Working Toward Ideals
The eleventh house is ruled by both Saturn and Uranus. Ideally, the Uranian aspect associated with working toward a just, equitable, and inclusive society dominates. However, this ideal is not easily achieved because the entrenched Saturnine and Plutonian forces fight to maintain the status quo, often camouflaging their powerplays behind "progressive" ideas that support their own interests.

Idealism and Polarization
Naive idealism is often thwarted by the absence of realistic programs that could facilitate desired changes. Rigid attitudes at both ends of the spectrum crystallize into polarization, which impedes action and maintains the existing power structures. Thus transformation is often slow and tedious. It is hard to see the light at the end of the tunnel, but there is nowhere else to go than toward the exit.

Maintaining Personal Balance
Saturn and Pluto in the eleventh house remind us that to maintain our own sanity and individuality, we must monitor the extent to which our values align with the group values. Alignment is critical. We make adjustments or leave the group.

We must also pay attention to the energy it takes for us to participate. If we overextend ourselves, we limit what we can contribute and accelerate the moment when we must leave and re-establish connection with ourselves.

How We Deal with Reality and Life's Challenges

I am future-oriented and strive to be free from the constraints and dysfunctions of the past.
I go out on a limb to make a difference.

I bravely offer my unique contribution.

I experiment with novelty and pursue my ideals.
I am willing to fail, be criticized, and not be taken seriously or heard.
With tenacity and commitment, I hold on to my vision and work on my mission.

The Sequence

Something valuable is gained while we actively engage in community, working toward common goals. But sometimes we lose ourselves in the eleventh house and Aquarian activities. Burnout in the eleventh house can be caused by too many activities and the stress of over-committing.

We may also become disillusioned and feel that there are just too many hurdles to accomplishing our goals. Even when progress is slow, we don't give up the vision, just our aggressive approach. Pisces offers us another strategy.

Twelfth House/Pisces: Connection to a Higher Power

In the twelfth house, we disengage from group activities and re-engage with our inner world and spiritual life.

The Twelfth House and Pisces

Pisces and its ruler Neptune open us to the higher knowledge of saints and mystics — what cannot be accessed through the intellect.

Transcendent Love
Neptune, the higher octave of Venus, transcends the physical and is not focused on relationships and feeling good through earthly situations and things. The Venus archetype represents objectified love, beauty, order, and harmony in physical reality. Neptune's love is without object. It is eternal, compassionate to all, selfless, and not possessive.

Our Inner, Spiritual Reality
In the twelfth house and Pisces territory, it is our inner, not our outer, reality that matters. We invest time and attention in our emotional life. We reflect on our life from an unattached, soul, and cosmic perspective, assessing what is and is not working and letting go of situations, relationships, and ideas that are holding us back. Our spiritual life takes center stage.

Subtle Sensitivity Awakens Us to a Higher Power
The Pisces and Neptune influence causes us to become more introspective, listen to our intuition, and tune in to our feeling sensitivity. In subtle ways, we cultivate a relationship with the cosmos, feel supported, and know that we are not alone. Even if not much seems to change in our outer life, when we connect with a higher power, shifts happen in ways we can't expect or plan for.

Ultimately, it is our relationship with a higher power that makes it possible to survive and thrive in life. In neutral detachment, we are able to stay centered and take care of ourselves when around unbalanced and confrontive people. We align with a spiritual force through compassion, forgiveness, and oneness. We can stand for what is right from a neutral position of acceptance.

Issues to Deal With
In the twelfth house and Pisces territory, we can fall prey to gullibility, disillusionment, and unrealistic expectations. Pisces is prone to lack boundaries and is often an empath with acute sensitivity to the suffering and needs of others and Mother Earth. Pisces's natural selflessness, compassion, and willingness to give, sacrifice, and serve can lead to too many commitments and a lack of attention to one's personal needs.

The Pisces Twelfth House Challenge
The basic challenge in the twelfth house is to actually connect with a higher power and then trust and surrender to IT. Our ego/personality-driven experiences in the world still exist. We can't escape into a cave and isolate ourselves. And even if we could, we would be lured by escapism, a chance to avoid responsibility, and be unable to connect.

Let Go and Let God
Optimally, the twelfth house is one of spiritual reconnection, physical rehabilitation, and energy recharging. The only thing that brings us peace and connection is to "Let go and let God."

Spiritual Awakening
Authentic spiritual awakening leads to profound insights and a total remake of our worldview and approach to both life and death. We can then live in an experience of our divine identity. We can enjoy the fact that each one of us is unique and one with all of existence.

Saturn and Pluto in the Twelfth House and Pisces Territory

Saturn and Pluto transits in the twelfth house and Neptune transits in any of the houses can create confusion, uncertainty, and breakdowns, which can be dealt with only by connecting to, trusting, and surrendering to a higher power. Ultimately, we must give up illusionary pursuits and surrender to the reality of divine love.

Addictions and Emotional Chaos
Saturn and Pluto transits in the twelfth house and those involving Pisces and Neptune anywhere in our birth chart get our attention through chaos, scandal, addictions, and various forms of emotional malaise, including depression. Those who don't acknowledge the presence and preferences of their emotions express their emotions in covert ways and through addictions. A main driver of addictions is the inability and unwillingness to deal with the harshness of physical reality. The problem is that addictions suppress feelings and take us out of the body, making it harder to deal with physical reality.

More Time with Ourselves
When Saturn and Pluto enter the twelfth house, we want to limit or eliminate demanding activities. Our deep desire now is to spend more time with ourselves so we can get to know

ourselves at a deeper level and cultivate our connection with a higher power. We distance ourselves from others so we can let go of outside attachments and return to our personal womb where we can be rebirthed into the world of oneness.

We want and need time to be alone to connect with our inner reality and the Source of our being. We seek alone time to shift gears from the externally oriented phase of our life in the eleventh house and to enjoy awakening to the nonphysical realms.

Clean Out and Empty Ourselves
We divest ourselves of what is no longer useful — both physical objects and emotional defenses. We empty ourselves so we can be filled with divine guidance and grace.

Yearn to Connect with the Divine
At this stage, we yearn to connect with the Divine. We trust that our soul will guide us into the future. The unknown becomes our best friend. As boundaries are dissolved, we don't lose ourselves; we find ourselves.

Pluto and the Dark Side
When Pluto is in the twelfth house, we want to connect with a higher power, but we may get lost in the traps and diversions of life's many distractions and forms of addiction. We may seek substitutes for the real connection when we don't know how to authentically connect and experience our oneness. Basically, we seek ways to not feel our pain and anguish. We numb ourselves to life, our body, and the Divine.

Avoid Illusions to Find Reality
Pluto does not let us make up fantasies and excuses that prevent us from an authentic experience. We have to become friends with emptiness even when our initial experience of coming face-to-face with our dark, unillumined inner space is scary. But in this vast space, we connect to Source and find our eternal soul. Illusions must be given permission to fall away to awaken to infinite reality.

Mental activity and projections (thinking too much!) block our experience of reality, which is always available to become known. But we have to make ourselves available to know it! We miss what is there when we burden ourselves with false realities and cover up the experience with drugs, alcohol, and sugar.

Fatal Fantasies or Divine Embrace?
Pluto and Saturn in the twelfth house remind us that the twelfth house is sometimes termed the house of suffering. It is associated with fate and karma, hospitals, and prisons.

Unevolved Pisces chooses escapism and illusion (including bingeing any form of entertainment media) to avoid dealing with life's inherent difficulties and to opt out of seriously engaging in the work necessary to establish and maintain divine connection.

From Pisces's and Neptune's perspective, the ultimate way through all life's difficulties requires a relationship with the Divine. Connecting with the sacred makes it possible to find security and peace within. The way out is within. Joy and liberation are found in service of the collective welfare. Through our relationship with a higher power, we experience unconditional love and unity, and find what we are all ultimately seeking.

Positive Potentials Awakened
The good news is that Saturn transits in our twelfth house can offer us the grounding to manifest our goals. As our creativity is unleashed and our intuitive knowing is more realistic, our visions can become reality.

How We Deal with Reality and Life's Challenges

I connect to and cultivate my relationship with a higher power.
I know I'm never alone.
I accept the way things turn out. I relax and do my best.

I trust a higher power and can ask for and receive guidance and help.
There is a pathway through every problem.
God is in charge. I am a humble servant.

The Sequence

I keep going.
I am grateful for my life and every breath.

Embracing Our Earth School Journey

Although certain arenas of life demand more attention and are focal points for our personal growth and expression, our human life takes us on a journey through all 12 houses.

While we are on planet Earth, there is always pressure, questions, more to explore, more to become, more ways to participate, and more to digest, integrate, and enjoy. We are better off if we get used to and accept this nature of Earth School and embrace all aspects of life while we are here. We won't be here forever. There will never be another you or a life like yours

Chapter 12:
2020 Is a New Beginning

It is important to appreciate the unique nature of the year 2020, when three new astrological cycles begin. The rare alignments of Jupiter, Saturn, and Pluto in Capricorn mark the ending of an era and the birth of a new, yet unexplored and undefined, world. Collectively and individually, we are all impacted and invited to participate in our own unique way.

A Critical Turning Point

The three 2020 conjunctions signal a turning point and portend fundamental changes in many aspects of life as we know it. Something profound is happening. We are both witnesses and participants.

What we believe, our philosophy of life, and how we define reality are all being challenged. We are at a critical evolutionary juncture. The dark shadow side of our beliefs, institutions, and emotions is being exposed. As the frequency of the Earth rises, anything that does not resonate with the heart will be brought into the light to be transformed. The brighter the light, the darker the shadow. The more conscious we become, the more aware we are of what has previously been hidden, suppressed, and denied.

Pivotal Times

Saturn and Pluto energies in Capricorn can cause us to feel overwhelmed. Paradoxically, we want to hold on, but to move forward, we have to stop resisting and accept inevitable change. We can be afraid of change because we believe we like things the way they are. But are we really comfortable with the status quo? A more appropriate goal is to be able to handle whatever life brings from a mature, neutral perspective.

These transition times from the Piscean to the Aquarian Age are challenging to say the least. We are dealing with the death rattle of duality and the birth pangs of unity. The rewards are great if we release old patterns and limited beliefs. We can gain a deep sense of inner peace, wholeness, and joy by living in heart-centered consciousness. As we awaken to our interconnectedness with all life, we are able to enjoy and appreciate life at a whole new level.

Uncertainty Is the New Norm

In 2020, we will be riding the waves of turbulent, unclear waters, which are characteristic of transitions between the old and the new. And there are three (3!) new cycles beginning in 2020!

A deep desire for change is brewing, but what we want is difficult to articulate in practical terms and doable options. We are caught between idealizing future outcomes and longing for an idealized past. The future will probably be significantly different than we can even imagine.

As previous economic and social certainties evaporate, political leaders may try to appease and appeal to feelings of uncertainty and desperation by promising a return to the "good old days" or a magical revamp that skips the tedious process of transformation.

The new norm is uncertainty and even chaos. The current chaos-drama may just be the beginning of very turbulent times.

Pluto — From Fear to Love

The major player Pluto is about necessity, not comfort. Pluto represents power that is not under our conscious control. The Pluto process is about becoming conscious of fear-based subterranean forces that control us so that we can release ourselves from their grip. Pluto represents the deep impulse to release the programs and beliefs that enslave us so that we can be free. This is a lifelong process that just keeps going, one layer at a time. The payoff is that we find a more authentic and purified self. We release fear and awaken to love.

When planetary energies align in certain ways, we are ready to be "reborn," and it becomes easier to release the past. A dormant power awakens that is ready to be lived. We are living in one of those times when cosmic forces are facilitating our renewal and awakening.

Awakening to a New Life

Pluto is about an awakening, a new life, a new worldview, a transformed reality. Some may give lip service to these ideas. But both on the collective and personal levels, we are often more interested in maintaining a comfortable, or even an uncomfortable, status quo.

However, as my mother Ruth demonstrated in the way she lived her life, we are each at choice in how we use the energies available at any time. We can choose how we view the world and our role in it. The 2020 conjunctions offer us a chance to renew and redesign how we wish to live our life. Saturn offers a chance to bring our dreams into physical reality. The presence of both Saturn and Capricorn makes this a very practical and creative conjunction.

Deeper Causes, Trends, and Truths

Surprising events do not come out of nowhere. Game-changers surface from deeper underlying factors that have reached a tipping point. If we are shocked, it is because we have lived in denial and chosen not to see what was brewing before our eyes. Change is difficult, but ignorance exacts a greater price.

When shocking events like 9/11 happen, we can refuse to look deeply at possible causes, or we can look for a scapegoat and abdicate any responsibility. We are always at choice as to how we interpret events in both our collective and personal lives. Our tendency is to resist acknowledging the deeper truths that Pluto exposes. Too often we choose not to see even the most obvious truths. When we favor denial, the events around Saturn-Pluto can push us into reaction instead of moving us forward.

"Wakeup calls," intense events or experiences, happen for a reason — to help us awaken to the light within and then be the light and to embody peace wherever we find ourselves.

It Is Not "Them"

The famous Pogo cartoon quote, "We have met the enemy and he is us," offers us deep wisdom.

The dark force that is ruling the world may be our own fear. External authorities will always wield power over us if we are controlled by fear and project our fear onto them. When we feel powerless, we want simple solutions and guaranteed certainties. We pay the price by accepting what "authorities" tell us to think and believe. Not having to think for ourselves gives a certain sense of security, but it also makes us into docile sheep.

Feeling powerlessness around authority is a normal human instinct. But connecting to our own power and the power of love is what Saturn and Pluto are about.

Pluto's job is to make us realize how controlled and manipulated we are. The power structures don't want us to rock the boat. But most of us don't want to rock our private boat either. We may like it when things get stirred up a bit and give us some hope, but who is willing to capsize their own boat for deep transformation?

Cutting Through Ideologies and Exploring Ideas

The issues we face are complex. There are no simple answers. Comprehensive solutions are necessary and difficult. For example, providing an equal education for all, which requires adequate funding to raise the quality of substandard schools, also involves addressing a number of other key issues. These include poverty, homelessness and lack of affordable housing, violence at home and in our communities, food insecurity and junk food-based diets, and being raised by a single working parent — all of which make it difficult for students affected by these conditions to learn.

Taking sides, focusing on one aspect of any complex problem, demonizing everyone else, and arguing about who is right and who is wrong don't address the real issues. Polarized battles engage us in emotionally charged dead ends, accomplish nothing useful, feed anger, increase negativity, build resentment, and distance us from solutions.

When we identify with dogmatic positions instead of learning from our personal experience and integrating it into our own philosophy of life, we aren't authentically ourselves. Lost in the chaotic rumblings of our mind, we aren't present to our own life or soul.

When simplistic ideologies hijack our values and conversations, we ignore the relevant facts and live in denial of real-life reality. Human heart-to-heart connection is where we can identify common ground and work together to improve the situation.

The 2020 Rite of Passage

Our 2020 encounters and challenges can be summarized as a *rite of passage*. We all have our own interpretations that go with our life story forged from the dynamics and demands of family, societal influences, education, and economic position. The 2020 rite of passage takes place when we take responsibility for own life and consciously notice and become accountable for what and how we create. 2020 is about choosing how we wish to define and direct the next decade of our life.

Long-Term Process

On the physical plane, destruction is quick and easy. Reconstruction and creation in physical reality take time, resources, and effort. If our house has been burned down, it takes time to build a new house and a new life. In the physical world, there are no quick fixes or free lunches. We are in this for the long haul.

Recognizing that we are engaged in evolutionary transformation that is slow and often tedious, we can choose to be part of a long-term process of building new foundations, which make it possible to create a more equitable, just, and peaceful world.

A shift in mass consciousness is a slow process, but it is achieved by individuals waking up, becoming more conscious, and uplifting themselves, each other, and the collective consciousness from fear into compassion, light, and love.

Wise Choices and Use of Energy

It is critical at this time to wisely choose how we use our energy and not dissipate it with negativity, doubt, and inaction. Succumbing to the fear and negativity that supports the current power structures wastes our precious energy, which is better applied to engaging in constructive conversations, analysis, wise choices, commitment, and action.

Life Will Never Be the Same Again

Many are saying that after 2020 life will never be the same again. There are so many conjectures about what could happen, from the alienation of automation to alien invasions, from turmoil to transformation. Everything is possible. But we can be sure that outcomes will be dramatically different depending upon whether we live from mental conflict and fear or focus on connecting with and trusting a higher power and our own heart.

The Truth Is Peace and Love

As Mahatma Gandhi once said, "To believe in something, and not to live it, is dishonest." Yet at the same time, it is hard to tell the truth because then we would have to admit that we have been living a lie.

Many aspects of the current global systems are cruel, corrupt, criminal, and dishonest. This situation is a product of human fantasies, aggressive egos, and competitive greed gone wild. How can those who care help lead the way toward a better, more heart-centered future?

We must walk the truth, not just talk about it. The truth is peace and love, and it is present within each of us. With our own compassionate rebirth, we can reshape our society and its systems to serve love and peace.

A Decade Lived from Our Heart

In the Aquarian Age, our evolutionary imperative is to find our center in our heart and to practice living with compassion. We are being compelled to reorganize our psyche to become conscious of the true nature of our being, which is love.

Life is rich, its expressions infinite, and its options unlimited. 2020 is about designing the next decade of our life and beyond. The more we embrace ourselves and manage our life from our hearts, the happier and more at peace we will be.

2020 is about an awakening, a new life, a new worldview, a transformed reality, and embracing ourselves and our life with courage and compassion.

Appendix 1: Understanding Your Birth Chart

Our Birth Chart Is Our Soul Blueprint

Our soul chooses to be born when the Sun, Moon, and planets are in the exact location that corresponds to the energies and their dynamic interaction that will serve us in this incarnation. The location of the celestial bodies at the time of our birth is visually represented in our birth chart. Our personality, soul, and life's journey are all encoded in our birth chart.[28]

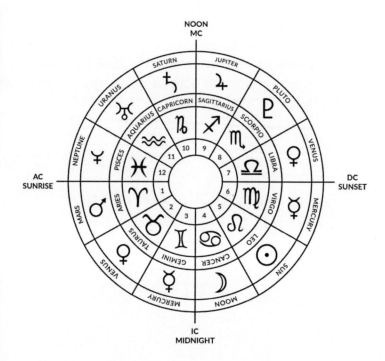

Our birth chart denotes the *invisible blueprint of our soul's journey.* Since we cannot see our inner-being in a mirror, like we can see our physical body, our birth chart can serve as a guiding tool in our human incarnation. Our birth chart indicates (1) the energies we have to work with, (2) what we are here to accomplish, (3) the nature of the challenges we face, and (4) our formula for finding courage, happiness, peace, and fulfillment in this life.

Our birth chart is encoded with the formula of the potentiality of universal energies that we were born to express. It is the blueprint of how our soul self operates and fits into the cosmic universal field.

Our personal astrology and the themes that play out during our lifetime are set the moment we are born. The planets, their zodiac signs, and their house placement guide us to a deeper understanding of who we are and what we are here to learn. Studying our natal chart helps us explore our predispositions, cultivate our unique attributes, and discover the voice of our soul.

---

[28] The following is excerpted and expanded from *The Inner Art of Kundalini Yoga: Awaken Your Heart to Love.* Chapter VI, "The Energetic Blueprint of Your Soul," examines how to identify the nature of the energies represented in your birth chart (polarities, modalities, and elements). Get your PDF e-book today at www.yogatech.com.

Attitude and Self-Discovery

It is important to view our birth chart with a positive and explorative attitude. Some people are afraid of what they might find. This is not an appropriate attitude. We want to use our birth chart to facilitate self-discovery and enrich our life's journey, to validate and find out more about ourselves, and to cultivate self-love.

We are engaged in a lifelong exploration and awakening of our soul self. By studying each archetype and the role it is playing in our life, we can incorporate its powers into our being.

The Zodiac Archetypes

Our human lessons can be categorized according to the 12 zodiac archetypes, which help us understand how the universal energies play out in our life.[29]

Each sign of the zodiac represents a path to fulfillment. The 12 signs provide us with 12 keys to access the potentialities and power of our soul. Each one denotes an archetypal combination of universal energies, which manifest as *specific challenges, moods, desires for expression, and needs for fulfillment.*

Although we each have our own special blueprint, we all work with the same archetypal energies. Every sign of the zodiac embodies a set of lessons that we must all learn in order to optimally operate in physical reality and to leave this Earth having evolved to a higher state of consciousness. As we mature and learn to work with the various challenges and lessons, we evolve and are able to access the powers and the gifts of each sign.

We can take advantage of the inflow of cosmic energies to (1) look at ourselves, others, and the world in new ways; (2) acquire deeper insights about ourselves and the Universe; and (3) propel ourselves to a more profound state of awareness and self-realization.

Planets		Zodiac Signs	
Sun	☉	Aries	♈
Moon	☽	Taurus	♉
Mercury	☿	Gemini	♊
Venus	♀	Cancer	♋
Mars	♂	Leo	♌
Jupiter	♃	Virgo	♍
Saturn	♄	Libra	♎
Uranus	♅	Scorpio	♏
Neptune	♆	Sagittarius	♐
Pluto	♇	Capricorn	♑
Chiron	⚷	Aquarius	♒
North Node	☊	Pisces	♓
South Node	☋		
Axes			
Rising Sign	ASC	Descendent	DS
Midheaven	MC	Nadir (Imum Coeli)	IC

As we study the energetic makeup of each zodiac sign, we discover that the biggest challenges presented by each sign are also the source of their unique power and fulfillment. The key to finding resolutions to their specific issues is to learn to work with their energies. The

---

[29] For a detailed description of each of the 12 zodiac archetypes and their corresponding houses and planet including (1) arena of life, (2) human lessons and soul gifts, (3) soul goals, (4) sensory experiences, and (5) touchstones, see *The Inner Art of Kundalini Yoga: Awaken Your Heart to Love*, pp. 101-107. Also see Guru Rattana's *New Millennium Being* e-zines and Guru Rattana Blog at https://www.newmillenniumbeing.com and https://www.yogatech.com/Guru_Rattana_Blog/.

appropriate activation, balance, and integration of energies allow us to move out of pain, suffering, and dysfunctional patterns into liberating and empowering expressions of the archetypes and our soul.

My approach to the zodiac signs is to investigate their expression in terms of *asleep, waking up,* and *awakened consciousness.* There are no "bad" characteristics, just lessons that we must learn and attributes that we can cultivate to access and enjoy the power and potential of each sign and planet and thus our unique self.

We can relate to each zodiac sign and planet as a universal archetype that is available to come alive within us, assisting us on our path of self-discovery and self-love.

Houses of the Zodiac

The 12 houses in a birth chart each represent different phases and arenas of our human journey, including circumstances and environments where events and learning play out in our life experiences. Each house is associated with a zodiac sign and planet.

An empty house does not mean lack of activity but the absence of serious problems and more freedom of action. In houses with planets, there are more vital issues and life challenges.

Rising Sign and Placement of Planets in the Houses

The degree and sign at the horizon at our time of birth is our *rising sign,* or *ascendant*, which is the cusp of the first house, or the very beginning of our journey. Our time of birth determines our rising sign, which in turn determines the placement of the planets in the 12 houses.

The birth chart is like a 24-hour clock with the top representing 12 noon; the bottom, midnight; the left side, sunrise, or ascendant; and the right side, sunset, or descendant.

Our Sun will be located at the time of the chart that corresponds to our birth time. For example, if we were born at noon, our Sun will be at the very top of our chart. If we were born before noon, our Sun will fall in the eleventh house. If we were born after noon, our Sun will be in the ninth, eighth, or seventh houses. If we were born at midnight, our Sun will be at the nadir at the bottom of the chart. If we were born after midnight, our Sun will be in the third house. If we were born before midnight, our Sun will be in the fourth house. Obviously, the Sun of later births falls in subsequent houses.

Thus, unless we have Aries rising, the planets and their zodiac sign will bring another energy to that house. For example, if we have Scorpio rising and planets in Scorpio in the first house, both the Aries nature of the first house and the planets in Scorpio are influential factors.

Planets

The planets each represent a fundamental aspect of human life. A *bundle pattern* of many planets grouped together in the same sign or house indicates a concentration of energies in specific areas of our life, often excluding other areas.

Retrograde Planets ℞

When a planet is retrograde, its energy is turned inward and is thus more personal and subjective. The full, active power of the planet is less available for action in the outer world. Those with many retrograde planets in their birth chart are often more introspective and less action-oriented than those with most or all of their planets moving forward. Retrograde planets are common in the charts of geniuses. ℞ is the retrograde symbol, which will appear under the planet on the birth chart.

Because the retrograde planets move more slowly, their messages may be easier to perceive. Retrograde slows down manifestation, not because things won't happen, but because more thinking and preparation are involved. Action may be delayed, but not denied.

The Sun and Moon are never retrograde.

Our Sun and Moon

The very first things we want to explore are the energies of our Sun and Moon because they are the two most influential players in our birth chart.

Sun ☉
How we shine our light from our heart, conscious will.

Our Sun is the basic soul energy that permeates our being. Our light shines the energy of our Sun sign. We are most conscious of our Sun sign energy, which we must learn how to deal with first and foremost. Our Sun represents our will, individuality, spirit, and sense of identity. Our Sun sign is the *foundation of our self or our active masculine will.*

Moon ☽
Nature of our emotions, unconscious will.

Our Moon represents the *emotional feeling side* of our being. Our *instincts, subconscious patterns,* and *inner, feeling nature* are expressed through our Moon. This part of our being may be hidden, but we must always remember that to a large extent it is in charge. Our subconscious emotional imprints and programming can sabotage the best laid plans of our active will and ideas about how things "should be."

We discover and develop our Sun sign. We retrieve, own, acknowledge, and heal our Moon sign.

The Personal Inner Planets

The personal planets — Mercury, Venus, and Mars — move through the zodiac in about one year. These are also known as the inner planets because they orbit closest to the Sun. They symbolize aspects of our personal identity.

Because the nature of their influence shifts quickly compared with the slower outer planets, they do not play a significant role in defining new long-term cycles. However, their zodiac sign and house placement in our birth chart are important in identifying aspects of our human makeup.

Mercury ☿
Our mind, how we think, and mode of communication.

Mercury represents how our mind operates, looks for, and analyzes information. It helps determine how we communicate and understand what others are saying as well as the nature of the activities we like. Mercury is our messenger that moves between different realities: subconscious, unconscious, conscious, nonverbal, and nonphysical.

Venus ♀
What we love, what makes us feel loved, how we love. What makes us feel safe, comfortable, at peace, and at ease. Feminine, flowing, nurturing energy.

Venus represents our feminine/feeling energy, what we love, what we attract, and what makes us feel comfortable, peaceful, and harmonious.

Mars ♂
Active, masculine, action energy. What we choose to do. How we decide to use our creative energy. Decisive and dominant in terms of choices.

Mars represents our male energy, as in where and how we focus and direct our action.

Transitional Planets, Chiron, and the Nodes

Jupiter, Saturn, and the asteroid Chiron orbit the Sun beyond planet Earth and serve to link our human experience up with the outer planets.

Jupiter ♃
How we expand, evolve, and transform beyond our current reality. What takes us out of ruts and makes us feel free and on purpose. Adds a social element or desire to connect.

Jupiter represents what motivates us to go beyond our current or perceived limitations. When we do, we are successful and pleased with ourselves.

Saturn ♄
The nature of the lessons we must learn this lifetime. What seems difficult, slow, and taxing. How we manifest and bring our dreams into reality.

Saturn represents our challenges and life lessons that we must learn to become mature adults and to be able to manifest and take care of ourselves in physical reality.

Chiron ⚷
What we must heal this lifetime. Involves a wound that must be understood, accepted, and forgiven.

Chiron is one of the currently used five asteroids (mini planets). Chiron orbits between the inner and outer planets, specifically between Saturn and Uranus. Chiron represents what we must heal to be empowered and to move into our planetary service. The healing is the source of our personal empowerment and requires self-love.

North Node ☊
New territory for the evolution of our soul this lifetime. May seem unfamiliar and foreign.

The North Node represents what we have to learn this lifetime. We have to embrace this energy and its lessons. This is new territory that must be explored to be successful and make evolutionary progress in this lifetime.

South Node ☋
The sign directly opposite the North Node (and usually not given on the birth chart). Familiar territory. The foundation that must be developed for the awakening of the North Node.

The South Node is what we have already learned or the talents that we have acquired in previous lives. We find "relearning" these skills easier and use them as a foundation for moving into the unknown arena of our North Node. The North and South Nodes are always exactly opposite each other and in complementary signs.

Impersonal Outer Planets

The impersonal planets are Uranus, Neptune, and Pluto. They are also known as the outer planets because of their distance from the Sun. It takes them 6, 12, and 18 years (respectively and approximately) to orbit around the Sun. Each time a planet orbits the Sun, it changes signs. Thus, the outer planets stay in the same sign of the zodiac for approximately 6-, 12-, and 18- plus years.

The outer planets define generations because all those born in the same 6-, 12-, or 18-plus-year cycle will have their outer planets in the same sign. The outer planets impact people in the same age group simultaneously and confront us with similar lessons. The energies and the challenges of the outer planets, being more distant, are harder to access and understand than those of the inner planets.

Uranus ♅

Unexpected, unpredictable, and even shocking ways that we wake up.

Uranus is the wakeup/surprise planet. It represents where and how we search for freedom, uniqueness, and revolutionary change. Uranian wakeup calls lead to freedom and break the bonds of conventionality so we can build our personal identity.

Neptune ♆

How we dream. The nature of our illusions and source of deception. How we express our divine gifts and connection with the Divine.

Neptune represents where and how we search for the Divine.

Pluto ♇

The nature of our deep inner transformation. How we wake up to subconscious programming and release it.

Pluto represents our instinctual drive toward evolutionary transformation, death, and rebirth.

Ascendant and Angles

Ascendant — Rising Sign (A^{SC})
The lens through which we see the world. The meaning we look for and give to what we see. How we perceive reality.

Our ascendant, or rising sign, is the sign that is on the cusp of the first house. The ascendant represents our first impression of the world and the lens through which we continue to view it. The ascendant represents our temperament and physical body. It also describes the nature of our reactions to daily pressures and how we deal with circumstances and our immediate surroundings. Usually, unbeknownst to us, others perceive us in terms of our ascendant.

For example, with Scorpio rising, we will take life seriously and need to find deep meaning in our activities. Leo rising will look for and find satisfaction in fun and heart-centered activities.

Descendant (D^S)
The sign directly opposite the ascendant that is on the cusp of the seventh house or house of relationships.

The planets and their signs in the seventh house give us information about the challenges we face, what we want and attract, and what plays out in our relationships with friends and partners. For example, with Aries on the cusp of and in the seventh house, we will attract confrontation and probably like it, until we honor equally our own identity and needs and those of our partner.

Midheaven (M^C)
The sign at the very top of the chart: 12:00 noon. How we present ourselves to the world and how we are seen.

On the cusp of the tenth house, the zodiac sign on our midheaven indicates how we feel self-assured in the world and what we must work on to gain hard-earned recognition for our contribution to the world. For example, with Virgo on our midheaven, we need to feel self-sufficient and be an independent "priest" or "priestess" to gain respect and serve as a role model in the world.

Nadir or Imum Coeli (IC)
The sign at the very bottom of the chart: 00:00 midnight. The nature of our inner reality and how we must relate to our inner reality to find our emotional and sacred space within.

The zodiac sign of our nadir indicates the nature of both the divine and the devil that live in our inner reality. It defines how and what we have to be conscious of to build a sacred foundation for our inner space. For example, with Pisces at the nadir, we may be spaced out and ungrounded. As we connect to the infinite space within, we can feel cozy inside our body and nurtured by divine love.

> ***There are no "bad" characteristics,*** just lessons that we must learn and attributes that we can cultivate to access and enjoy the power and potential of each sign and planet and thus our unique self. We can relate to each zodiac sign and planet as a universal archetype that is available to come alive within us, assisting us on our path of self-discovery and self-love.

Appendix 2:
Decode Your Energetic Blueprint

Obtain a Copy of Your Birth Chart

To get a copy of your birth chart, you need to know the *date, time,* and *place* of your birth. There are free charts available online. If you do not know the exact time, be as accurate as you can. The ascendant and house positions are determined by the time and place of birth. For your energetic composition, the exact time is not as important.

There are endless ways to use your birth chart to explore the blueprint of your soul. *For your initial investigation, the most important things to identify are*

1. The basic energies of your Sun sign, Moon, and ascendant
2. The total energetic composition of your chart

Exercise One: Sun, Moon, and Ascendant

Identify the energetic nature of your Sun, Moon, and ascendant.

Polarities
M — Stable/Mind/Masculine (Fire and Air)
F — Flowing/Feeling/Emotional/Feminine (Water and Earth)

Modalities
G — Generate (Cardinal) - Initiating, taking action, coming up with ideas
O — Organize (Mutable) - Allowing, doing the work to make things happen
D — Deliver (Fixed) - Holding, keeping things together, enjoying

Elements
F — Fire
A — Air
E — Earth
W — Water

Exercise Two: Total Composition

The simplest way to identify the basic energies expressed in your birth chart is to find a program on the Internet that gives you this information, that is, the number of planets in each element and in each of the three modalities. (Cardinal = G, Mutable = O, Fixed = D). The numbers given are usually based on the primary planets. Your numbers will vary if you choose to include Chiron, the ascendant, and the nodes.

- ♥ Add fire and air to get the total of planets in Stable/Mind/Masculine.
- ♥ Add water and earth to get the total of planets in Flowing/Feeling/Feminine.

Use the charts below and on the next page to identify the following information. Count the number of planets you have in

Polarities
M — Stable/Mind/Masculine (Fire and Air)
F — Flowing/Feeling/Emotional/Feminine (Water and Earth)

Modalities
G — Generate
O — Organize
D — Deliver

Elements
F — Fire
A — Air
E — Earth
W — Water

And there you have it. That is the energetic blueprint of your soul! As you work with the nine universal energies, you will be able to better understand your gifts, challenges, and lessons. This is an illuminating way to get to "know thyself."

Energetic Anatomy of Zodiac Archetypes

Polarities	STABLE		FLOWING	
Elements	FIRE	AIR	WATER	EARTH
Modalities				
G—GENERATE	Aries	Libra	Cancer	Capricorn
O—ORGANIZE	Sagittarius	Gemini	Pisces	Virgo
D—DELIVER	Leo	Aquarius	Scorpio	Taurus

My Energetic Blueprint

Planet	Sign	Polarity M F	Modality G - O - D	Element E, W, F, A
Sun ☉ (conscious will)				
Moon ☾ (unconscious emotions)				
Ascendant A^SC (lens to view world)				
Mercury ☿ (mind and activities)				
Venus ♀ (what we love)				
Mars ♂ (active energy)				
Jupiter ♃ (what expands us)				
Saturn ♄ (lessons and manifesting)				
Chiron ⚷ (heal to be empowered)				
Uranus ♅ (freedom and individuality)				
Neptune ♆ (fantasies/Divine)				
Pluto ♇ (transformation)				
North Node ☊ (what we must learn)				
South Node ☋ (past experiences)				
PLANET TOTAL				

About Guru Rattana, Ph.D.

Groundbreaking author, teacher, and teacher of teachers, Guru Rattana has followed a committed spiritual path since the age of 25 when she started studying Hatha Yoga. In 1977, she met and began training in Kundalini Yoga with Yogi Bhajan and was one of the first KRI Certified Teachers. In the early 80s, Yogi Bhajan told her that she would be the teacher who brought the most students to Kundalini Yoga.

She is author of four of the original (now revised and updated) and still best-selling Kundalini Yoga and Meditation manuals, based on Yogi Bhajan's early classes. In her 11 books, she demystifies spiritual concepts and adds subtle feminine sensitivity to yoga traditions previously created by men for men. Each of her books contributes to elucidating the *Inner Art of Kundalini Yoga and Meditation.*

Her monthly *Guru Rattana Blog* explores topics in astrology, Kundalini Yoga, and spiritual awakening. Over 200 of her original astrological newsletters, *New Millennium Being*, are now available on https://www.newmillenniumbeing.com. In her profound and captivating teaching style, she elucidates the astrological archetypes and how to experience their powers using Kundalini Yoga in *Guru Rattana Online* streaming video service. Nearly 100 classes are available at https://www.yogatech.com/grol.

Her annual international teaching tours have taken her to 19 countries in Eastern and Western Europe, where she teaches *Inner Awareness Kundalini Yoga Teacher Training Courses* (registered with Yoga Alliance) and *The Gift of Womanhood* courses featuring her book with that title. She is lead trainer and co-creator of K.R.I.Y.A. (Kundalini Rising International Yoga Academy).

Following receipt of her M.A. from Johns Hopkins School of Advanced International Studies, Guru Rattana earned a doctorate in political science from the University of Geneva, Switzerland, and went on to pursue an academic career, teaching at Dartmouth College, MIT, New Hampshire College, US International University (San Diego), Stanford University, and the Institute for Transpersonal Psychology (Palo Alto). Her spiritual path has inspired her to write and teach about awakened heart consciousness to create the foundation for real political, social, and personal transformation.

Guru Rattana lives in Coronado (San Diego), California.

Books by Guru Rattana, Ph.D.

Transitions to a Heart-Centered World (2nd edition, 2014)
Comprehensive resource of early Kundalini Yoga sets and meditations of Yogi Bhajan, offering powerful techniques to help you open your heart to unconditional love.

Relax and Renew (2nd edition, 2017)
Takes stress reduction to the level of holistic resolution. The techniques offered in this book don't just cover up the symptoms — they help cure the problem!

Sexuality and Spirituality (2nd edition, 2018)
Revolutionary guide to spiritualize sexual energy to enjoy more depth and pleasure in sacred sex and relationships.

Introduction to Kundalini Yoga Vol. I - *Begin and Deepen Your Practice*; and Vol. II - *Inner Awareness and Self-Initiation* (2nd edition, 2015) The fundamentals and benefits of Kundalini Yoga and Meditation.

The Destiny of Women Is the Destiny of the World (2006)
An inspiring and invaluable handbook for woman to elevate her consciousness and celebrate her womanhood.

The Inner Art of Kundalini Yoga — Awaken Your Heart to Love (2011 as *Inner Art of Love*, 2019)
Learn to use the sacred technology of Kundalini Yoga and Meditation to connect with your inner reality, awaken your heart, and become a conscious soul-directed human being.

The Gift of Womanhood — Inner Mastery, Outer Mystery (2012)
Reveals woman's mysterious design and guides you to find your authentic identity as a sacred woman, using Kundalini Yoga techniques that awaken your soul.

The Power of Neutral — Soul Alchemy in Meditation (2013)
Outlines the keys to awakening and your inner journey, revealing how the mind works and practical ways to direct your meditation practice.

Your Life Is in Your Chakras (greatly expanded 2nd edition, 2014)
Unique collection of information, techniques, and teachings to develop the faculties and gifts of your chakras.

Sing to Your Soul — Awaken to Oneness: Jap-ji Explains the Spiritual Path (2016)
Decodes in poetic simplicity the essence of the spiritual journey.

How to Order Your Manuals, Books, DVDs, and CDs

Guru Rattana's manuals and a huge selection of Kundalini Yoga books, DVDs and CDs are available from the Yoga Technology Online Store, http://www.yogatech.com. There you will enjoy very competitive prices and rapid order fulfillment. Special wholesale terms are available for teachers who sign up for our Teachers' Forum.

You can also check out a sample streaming video and sign up for *Guru Rattana Online* Classes, discover a wealth of information about Kundalini Yoga, and read and subscribe to the *Guru Rattana Blog*.